YOU CAN'T MAKE THIS
STUFF UP

Also by Theresa Caputo

There's More to Life Than This

YOU CAN'T MAKE THIS STUFF UP

Life-Changing Lessons from Heaven

the

LONG ISLAND MEDIUM

THERESA CAPUTO

with

Kristina Grish

ATRIA BOOKS

New York   London   Toronto   Sydney   New Delhi

ATRIA BOOKS

A Division of Simon & Schuster, Inc.
1230 Avenue of the Americas
New York, NY 10020

First Atria Books hardcover edition September 2014

ATRIA BOOKS and colophon are trademarks of Simon & Schuster, Inc.

For information about special discounts for bulk purchases,

please contact Simon & Schuster Special Sales at 1-866-506-1949 or business@simonandschuster.com.

The Simon & Schuster Speakers Bureau can bring authors to your live event. For more information or to book an event contact the Simon & Schuster Speakers Bureau at 1-866-248-3049 or visit our website at www.simonspeakers.com.

Jacket design by Zoe Norvell
Jacket photography by Sherwood-Triart Photography

Manufactured in the United States of America

10   9   8   7   6   5   4   3   2   1

Library of Congress Cataloging-in-Publication Data

Caputo, Theresa, author.
    You can't make this stuff up : life-changing lessons from heaven / Theresa Caputo
with Kristina Grish. —First Atria Books hardcover edition.
        pages   cm. —(Atria nonfiction original hardcover)
    1. Spiritualism. 2. Life—Miscellanea. 3. Conduct of life—Miscellanea.
    4. Success—Miscellanea. I. Grish, Kristina, author. II. Title.
    BF1261.2.C37   2014
    133.9'1—dc23
                                                                        2014029468

ISBN 978-1-4767-6443-6
ISBN 978-1-4767-6445-0 (ebook)

For two of my beloveds, who earned their wings
as I wrote this book: my grandfather Walter J.
Wells, who I know is entertaining the angels with
his war stories. Give Gram a big kiss for me! And
for our boy Petey, who bathed our family in licks,
affection, and loyalty for nearly twelve years.
We all miss you, especially Louie.

For my close family, whose love, support, and
understanding allow me to continue on this
journey. And to my extended Team Caputo family,
for respecting and protecting my gift, and for
making Spirit a priority over "business as usual."

For my clients and readers, who grant me the
honor and privilege of channeling their loved ones
and who allow me to share their stories so that
others may heal.

For God and Spirit, who amaze and humble me
with new lessons every day.

Contents

contents

Introduction

One to Grow On

This is a book about life-changing lessons that will enrich your years and speak to your soul. And while you may not want some crazy medium telling you how to go about your business, you need to at least hear me out. Fair enough?

But before we go there, I want to tell you a little about myself, in case you don't watch my reality show, *Long Island Medium*, haven't been to one of my live experiences, or didn't read my first book, *There's More to Life Than This*. Who knows? Maybe you bought this on a lark because you liked the cover. Maybe you thought, *I like this woman's style. All that lilac and bling speak to me.* If so, me too! We already have that in common! See, this is going to be fun.

So, I've been sensing and feeling Spirit since a young age, which at the time included my guides and the souls of dead people like my great-grandmother, who I'd never met. As a child, I actually thought it was normal to see figures at the foot of my bed or hear voices when I was the only person in the room. Even so, it bugged me out. I had night terrors that caused me to scream like mad when I sensed Spirit's energy, and as I grew up, I often felt stressed and strange in my body. To cope, I taught myself to mostly suppress what I was experiencing. A boatload of phobias kicked in after that, and my nervousness escalated, so by the time I met my husband, Larry, I was a real mess. I had debilitating anxiety that crept into every part of my life—my marriage, friendships, and downtime that was supposed to be relaxing, like when I went on vacation or tried watching a movie. I couldn't do a lot of everyday activities without panicking, like drive in the rain or go to a birthday party. I constantly feared something bad would happen. It was a frightening and sometimes embarrassing way to live.

After many, many years of trying to manage my feelings on my own and with a therapist—and not making much progress—my mom's friend Pat Longo, who's a spiritual healer and teacher, put me on the road to resolving my issues. After just one session, she explained, as if it were the most typical thing in the world, that the anxiety I felt was related to the fact that I'm a medium and was suppressing Spirit's energy. Can you imagine? The least reassuring news you can give an anxious person is that dead people are drawn to them! But lo and behold, Pat was right.

I soon learned that I channel Spirit through my chakras, and when it enters my crown, or head, chakra, I need to release it through my words. So when Spirit tried for all those years to deliver their messages, their energy would channel through my crown, but I'd get scared and block it in my chest, causing my heart to race or my torso to feel heavy. I also learned that I am empathic, which means that the way I primarily communicate with Spirit is through sensing and feeling. So if, for instance, there was a soul that wanted to tell me they passed in a death connected to the throat or had trouble communicating toward the end of their life, I'd feel my throat close, which triggered very real panic attacks. You can see why this was hard to understand and get under control without the right kind of help.

Because I felt calmer after Pat's healing, I trusted her "diagnosis" and gradually learned how to control the energy around me. My anxieties became less dramatic, and I began to heal. After some hemming and hawing, I fully accepted my gift from God and devoted myself to helping others with my abilities. Soon I was channeling Spirit that included God, angels, guides, souls of faith like saints, and departed loved ones. I still sense and feel this Spirit today, but I've also created a "library" of signs and symbols based on my own personal experiences; these images help relay messages in a way you can connect with and interpret.

Pretty wild, right? Keep going. It gets better.

The Gist on Learning Lessons

Now, I know you're an adult who can love, hate, forgive, blame, appreciate, trust, and reject any person or opportunity you wish. But I also want you to realize there's a more purposeful and fulfilling way to navigate life's ups and downs. Spirit tells me that you're meant to lead a meaningful existence, here in the physical world, that's joyful and satisfies your soul. And they've guided me to the lessons that will show you how.

If you read my book *There's More to Life Than This*, you'll remember that Spirit says your soul exists on the Other Side before you're born and after you die, and the reason you're here at all is to learn lessons that enrich your journey and help your soul mature in the afterlife. Well, as my abilities have grown, I've noticed that many of the topics addressed during your readings can overlap, and Spirit has shown me that these are among the major lessons we're *all* meant to learn in this world. (When I channel your loved ones' souls, they tell me about their lessons too.) The good news is, you don't need a PhD in theology to realize that these lessons reflect Spirit's, especially God's, priorities. They're easy to understand and offer simple, decisive, and direct guidance. Most truths do.

Spirit's messages are life-changing, and their lessons are no exception. I think this is because both target the central issues that hold you back from healing and thriving at that moment. If you are new to a challenge, this immediately starts you on a journey to gaining perspective and feeling better; and if you can't get past hurdles or sticking points, Spirit tells you what to do to carry on. Bottom line, they know what works for you. They help you recognize what's in your heart and soul, and also what's missing, so you can embrace the life you desire. But since you can't always ask a medium for direction, Spirit wants you to be able to heed their advice on your own. You can do this by learning lessons that grow your soul and increase your awareness of what makes you feel whole.

As you read, you'll begin to appreciate that you're in the physical world to be taught lessons in various ways. You'll see that your life has a purpose, that things happen for a reason, and why, why, why. You'll find the lessons in your own incredible and difficult situations. And the more you accept direction, the more intimately you'll understand your soul and trust your intuition and guidance to show you, and keep you on, the spiritual path you're meant to follow.

Spirit, the Ultimate Collaborator

What's so astounding is that right after I decided to write a book about lessons, Spirit took its participation in this project to a whole other level. At my live shows, I noticed that similar struggles and experiences kept coming up in specific ways. So for example, in one night, I read three different people whose loved ones' souls congratulated them on losing weight; on another, I channeled multiple children killed by guns; and within a ten-day span, Spirit was really into blurting out when women were secretly pregnant against all odds. It was ridiculous! There were also more spiritual "themes," like angels, miracles, and inspiring dreams that made me stop and think. But what really blew my hair back—and that's saying a lot—was when people with related messages found each other after my shows to talk about their stories, exchange emails, laugh, hug, and just be there for one another. It's as if Spirit were organizing the book's material for me, while also creating a sense of community at my live events for the audience.

Then I began the writing process, and things got even nuttier. While deciding which stories to use, I couldn't believe how many causes of death repeated themselves. A few of the stronger souls had the same names too, which I feel was synchronicity getting my attention and confirming that I was on the right spiritual track (synchronicity is like a coincidence, but it's when two or more events that seem unrelated come together in a meaningful way). And when my coauthor and I got in touch with subjects for interviews or to follow up on a reading, nine times out of ten we happened to do so on a significant day, like the anniversary or birthday of the loved one we were discussing!

I never question Spirit, and my gut knew these unbelievable "coincidences" happened for a reason. Spirit always works in the most incredible and awe-inspiring ways. I believe Spirit made sure I realized that while we're all here to learn our own lessons, we share the challenges and triumphs that teach them to us. We learn from our lives and each other's, and this gives us hope that we can carry on in good and hard times. Our souls are connected in this world and the afterlife, so we're never really alone.

How to Use This Book

Early on, Spirit insisted that the book's chapters appear in a progressive, intuitive order. They didn't suggest how to organize them exactly, so I trusted my instincts. I knew the first lesson had to be about faith, and the final lesson about healing, because those two subjects truly bookend every spiritual learning process. In between, the lessons I included build on and inform each other, but you won't get lost if you jump around based on how you're feeling that day. I've also named each chapter according to a lesson that I feel Spirit wants you to know, but the main subjects of each (like patience, authenticity, love, gratitude, etc.) are what matter most. Finally, you'll notice that Spirit underscores the majority of their lessons with being the best person you can be, as you fulfill your journey, because your behavior has a sizable impact on others' lessons too.

Another thing that may stand out is that I talk a lot about God. As I've emphasized many times, and will continue to say, I call the most brilliant source of energy and the creator of the universe God because I was raised Catholic and this supports my faith. But Spirit tells me there is only one God, so if you want to call him a Higher Power or a name that is more closely aligned with your beliefs, have at it. I just don't want you to dismiss Spirit's lessons if you can't relate to my use of the G-word. You have to understand, it's impossible to write a book about lessons without talking about Him, since they all originate with Him and His intentions for your life on earth. I also want to be clear that although Spirit has said these are influential lessons for soul growth, I am in no way saying that you need to master these to "get into Heaven." I'm shown that everyone crosses over and then, depending on how well you completed your lessons, according to the path your soul determined before you were born, you enter the Other Side on a level that reflects those standards.

Last but not least, please don't think I'm the final word on spiritual lessons. I can only tell you what I've discovered that makes sense to me, and hope it resonates with you. More than anything, I think you'll find that this book is well worth the read for its amazing stories—*your* amazing stories. You'll laugh, you'll cry, you'll learn, and I guarantee you'll squeeze your loved ones a little tighter the next time you see them. Your grandma won't know what hit her!

1

Your Lessons Matter

Hey you, with the TV on in the background and the dog barking his freakin' head off: Are you paying attention here? Seriously—turn down the noise, get comfortable, and make yourself something to eat. While you're at it, make me a snack too. Sorry if I sound pushy, but I'm just excited to share the awesome lessons I've learned from Spirit that will help you embrace the life you're meant to live, and I want to make sure you're listening to what I'm about to say.

OK? You good now? Let's do this.

I'm a medium, but my job is about so much more than talking to dead people. I deliver healing messages from Spirit that can be life- and soul-changing experiences. I talk a lot about how Spirit's messages validate that they're loving, supporting, and guiding you from the Other Side, which I believe is Heaven. But what I don't always say is that these messages often contain essential lessons that can make your happiness grow and your soul thrive. Whether

1

Spirit presents the messages in a direct, subtle, or hysterical way, their words usually double as teachable moments for the person who's getting the reading, friends who hear about it later, and anyone else that's watching or listening in.

Spirit's told me that your soul chooses to live in the physical world many times to learn various lessons. These lessons help you to have a positive outlook and be of service to others. I also believe that you have an overarching lesson to learn in each lifetime, with smaller teachings folded into that journey. All your lessons tend to revolve around topics that make you a joyful and healthy person, including love, blame, faith, acceptance, sacrifice, forgiveness . . . that kind of thing. Given the powerful influence that these themes can have in your life here, it's no wonder Spirit makes me circle them over and over. And since I'm the only one who goes to all my readings, hello, I feel it's important to share Spirit's most compelling lessons with you. This way you don't miss out!

I think every person is searching for happiness, answers, and for things to make sense in life—basically, we're trying to learn the lessons. We look for sources of laughter, guidance, and unconditional love. We wrestle with fear, blame, regret, and oh my gosh, the guilt. We struggle with faith and gratitude, especially when signs and miracles don't seem to happen as often as we'd like. We look for a reason behind it all, and peace, no matter what we find, because these are the significant and revealing tasks we're meant to complete.

Why Bother to Learn Lessons?

I'm all for enjoying life to the fullest, so I don't want you to go through your day like you have one foot in the grave. But to understand why you should care about Spirit's lessons, both now and in the afterlife, you do need to recognize the role they play when you die and go to the Other Side.

Spirit tells me that when you pass, your soul peacefully leaves your body, and you're greeted by the souls of family and friends who died before you. You move toward a brilliant light I call God, but as I said earlier, if you want to call Him by another name like Higher Power, Yahweh, or Allah, go right ahead—God doesn't mind. On earth, you are a piece of God's energy, but in Heaven, your soul is one with His. You have a primary guide who's helped you throughout your life (some feel this is the same as a guardian angel) and who is there to greet you on the Other Side. With this main guide, your soul then reviews and evaluates the journey you had here, and you get to see how your actions affected others. While in a soul state, you experience what you made them feel, physically and emotionally, and how it related to your purpose in that lifetime.

During this life review, you're reminded that your soul chose its body, family, path, and purpose, and that learning lessons is why you went to the physical world in the first place. Basically, you learn lessons that enrich and mature your soul, with the ultimate goal of aligning with God's ways. But you also go for others, since your choices have a ripple affect; your journey impacts their happiness too, and a lot of what happens to you is part of a lesson for them. Another way you learn lessons is through people and events that force you to use the traits you're meant to acquire here. Marrying a sick spouse, for instance, might help you learn compassion, or choosing a handicapped body could teach you perseverance. Your lessons and purpose could also relate to advancing society somehow, like through humanitarian, artistic, scientific, or spiritual efforts. No matter what, we all come to the physical world to learn to be better people and souls.

On earth, you learn lessons faster than in Heaven, since life's obstacles and setbacks help you grow faster and more fully. Before your most recent journey began, your primary guide reviewed certain details of what it would be like; the basic outline came from God. You knew what some of your tests and experiences would be and maybe even prepared for them. You also discussed your purpose with your guide. Sometimes Spirit will reveal, during a reading, what a soul's purpose was if it will comfort the living. This might happen with an organ donor or an infant whose destiny was to pass from twin-to-twin transfusion syndrome (this is when a twin dies in utero, but its mom carries it to term so the living child can take in enough nutrients to survive). Once you're here, though, most people learn about their purpose through soul-searching. Finally realizing your purpose feels like one heck of a prize too. It'll make you happier than finding a plastic whistle in a Cracker Jack box!

Spirit's shown me that when you enter Heaven, you do this at a certain level, or point of spiritual growth, and that your life assessment is based on this level's criteria. A level is like a grade in school—the lower the level, the more lessons the soul has to learn. When your soul grows, it moves to new levels, and you have to finish one before moving higher or deeper into the next.

Levels are related to your soul's energy frequency, since this rises as you grow. Among other purposes, your frequency, also called a vibration, influences how well your soul communicates with the living after you die. Higher-level souls are better able to send more regular and harder-to-execute signs, like moving objects and futzing with electricity. They can also communicate more clearly with a medium. As for Hell, I'm not sure there is one, but I'm told that the souls of people who have learned few lessons and/or did serious harm in the physical world—think murder, abuse, deliberate evil—enter the Other Side at very low levels. They can become negative forces. I don't need to know where or how this energy source exists. I want nothing to do with negative energy of any kind.

When it's time to learn new lessons, your soul can do it in Heaven or reincarnate in a new body, with new experiences, in another lifetime. In every go-round, you have free will to make choices related to your lessons; you can choose one path or another, but they will all have the same general purpose and destiny. Throughout it all, God, guides, angels, souls of faith, and loved ones protect, direct, send messages, and intervene. They put people and situations in your path that prompt you to make decisions affecting future growth. Eventually you die, and it starts all over again.

If you can't be bothered to think about the afterlife while you're still kickin', it wouldn't kill you to learn lessons anyway. They're a huge part of what characterizes your soul, which is the core of who you are and aspire to be. No matter what your objective, making choices that satisfy your soul feels good.

Are You My Lesson?

Though some lessons might smack you in the face, be on the lookout for less obvious ones. I think most people assume that all lessons happen during major moments, like a heartbreaking death or beautiful soul mate reunion, because you feel their impact long after they happen. Certainly, losing a parent or gaining a best friend changes your life in an instant. But Spirit also tells me that we learn lessons in small, everyday interactions too. If you feel the urge to buy a stranger a cookie, say, or hold the door for a father lugging groceries, a diaper bag, and a car seat, everyone's day and souls benefit from that kindness.

On a more frustrating and stupid note, you know that jerk who took your seat on the bus? He could be a lesson in patience. How about your money-mooching brother? Generosity. Or your husband's friends who got pizza sauce on your couch during *Sunday Night Football*? Probably sacrifice. So the next time you're at Thanksgiving dinner, and your sister-in-law leaves you out of family photos, don't try to control, overanalyze, fight against it, or go cryin' in the bathroom, "Why is this happening to me, of all people?" Look for the lesson instead. Let the situation unfold, and find the reason. It helps you deal, and here's why: When the reason, and not the problem, becomes your focus, you don't think about how sad, pissed-off, or doomed you are. You can accept the outcome, then concentrate on how to move past it. Your life is your responsibility—your soul chose it long ago. If you want a positive and fulfilling journey, don't let people hold you back. And don't forget, Spirit is ready to intervene when you ask.

When I accepted my gift, God told me in so many words that He wants our

> *Your life is your responsibility—your soul chose it long ago. If you want a positive and fulfilling journey, don't let people hold you back. And don't forget, Spirit is ready to intervene when you ask.*

lives to be as rewarding and connected to each other as possible—but listen, this can't happen if you don't participate in your own happiness. Even when there's a tragedy, you can't let life happen to you when it's time to pick up the pieces. God gave you a beautiful, complex world in which to become a better, stronger, and happier you. And while painful situations can feel forced upon you, how you cope and work through them is a choice and, yup, usually a lesson.

So you know that saying "Everything happens for a reason"? Spirit's proven to me that it's not just for motivational posters and crocheted pillows! It's actually part of your soul's lessons and path. During readings, your loved ones' souls have told me that there's an order to why things occur the way they do, like when one person survives a car accident but another passenger dies, or when a child sees her deceased sister's spirit but other people can't. The literal answer to why these freaky examples happen is related to destiny and intuition. But if I dig deeper with Spirit, it might turn out that an accident victim's death inspired his family to work toward enacting tougher drunk driving laws, and the girl who saw Spirit comforted her grieving family with her stories. Talk about worthwhile reasons, not to mention great examples of how our souls learn and teach lessons to others!

I'm Like a Spirit CNN—All Lessons, All the Time

Spirit uses my abilities and platform in their lesson plans too, whether it's to help you find closure, fill in the blanks about a death, or even save a life. During a live show in Montreal, I read a woman whose son's best friend died in an off-roading accident.

The son was carrying such heavy survivor's guilt that the soul actually asked me to call his friend on the mom's cell phone during the reading! So with three thousand eavesdroppers in the theater, we put the young man on speakerphone. The soul told me that his friend "can't be with his soul right now"—which is what Spirit says when a person is considering suicide. A hush fell over the room, and no exaggeration, you could have heard a freakin' pin drop as we waited for his response.

The boy on the phone told me that he understood what Spirit meant and that he wouldn't take his life. Mom was beside herself with gratitude, and as I walked away, I couldn't ignore the crowd's murmurs. "Oh my God," said one lady, "she saved that boy's life." But you have to understand, it wasn't me who rescued anyone—it was Spirit. That soul used me as a messenger to remind this young man, who had his whole life ahead of him, that he needs to live the way God intended, according to the path that his soul chose. Suicide was not a solution to his grief. What struck me is that his lesson didn't only affect this one family; I sensed that Spirit reached other audience members who felt similarly desperate.

When it comes to teaching you lessons, your loved ones are eager to help. If your mother made a big deal over you when she was alive, do you really think she stops caring when she dies? If you've got work to do, her soul will continue to meddle and help your soul graduate to the appropriate level. A major reason for this is because your mom's soul is in what I call your "soul circle." Spirit says people in your world relive most lives with you, as relatives and friends, though your relationships to them change based on your lessons and purposes. Every person has a different role in each life, and those lives together create your soul's total experience on earth. You also don't play the same part in every life—your fiancé may have been a friend once, or your nephew might have been your mom!

Since they're in your soul circle, your loved ones feel invested in your growth, especially if they share your level. They root for you, since they know that the more you learn here, the less you need to do in Heaven. They have positive intentions, since they don't experience negativity that can cloud them. Helping you out also helps their souls grow. But more than anything, they lend a hand because they never stop loving you. Your bond literally lasts forever.

I've noticed that whatever soul's opinion matters the most to you, relative to what you're being taught, that's the soul that delivers your messages and lessons through me. A funny cousin might beat out a holy saint if you look up to Cousin Bob more! As long as you can place the messages in your life, that's all I care about. When I was ordering a char dog at the Weiner's Circle in Chicago, a famous hot-dog stand, a customer's dead mom's soul asked me to school her daughter about faith. I got the woman's attention by using the soul's *you-listen-here* voice, and though she didn't know me from a can of paint, she sure took note. "If my mama says go back to church," she said, "I'm goin' back to church!" Just like that, this woman's mama brought her closer to God. Lesson learned.

You know what I like to do when I get a rare moment to myself? Think about all the people in my life and what lessons we might be teaching each other. Try it sometime; it's a fun exercise! Like my mom and dad have shown me selflessness, since they both do a lot of volunteer work in our community. I've also learned a ton from my husband, Larry, who's made personal sacrifices so that I can use my gift to help people. I think he's gotten smarter from my abilities as well, because when he watches a live show or reading, he asks a million questions after! I know for a fact that our lessons and souls are deeply intertwined. That poor guy is stuck with me for eternity!

A Lesson for You, a Lesson for Me

When I read big groups, Spirit might work together to give the same message to a lot of people, which I call "piggybacking." When this happens, I ask that if you can relate to a message for someone else, accept it as also being from your loved ones. Souls that piggyback may not have been connected on earth, but they link up with "like-minded" souls when preparing for a group reading.

I mention this because Spirit has actually piggybacked during shows to teach me lessons too. For example, when my daughter, Victoria, got a tattoo, I didn't like that it was on her forearm—it's so visible! So when I saw it, I yelled at her and told her how disappointed I felt. I was pretty harsh, especially since Victoria got it when she was stressed out about living on her own, starting a new semester at college, and dealing with guys and nasty girls. Yet over the next few days, Spirit led me to channel an insane number of kids that couldn't deal with their own pressures, which led to depression, which led to using substances that helped them relax, which led to death. *Boom*, just like that, I took this as a nudge from Spirit that Victoria's getting a tattoo was a frigging gift. It was also a lesson about perspective and losing my temper—two recurring themes in my life, if you haven't guessed.

I felt awful about coming down so hard on V, but I try to

look at mistakes as lessons learned. Handling a situation poorly helps me make better choices next time. No bad experience is wasted, and you can't change the past. I feel every aspect of life is necessary, especially when you screw up or fall apart, because you get smarter and become more aware. And if you repeat the same error a few times? Eh, I think of it like training for a fitness goal. Ten screw-ups are like doing ten burpees in the hard-core workout of Life—they whip you into shape. It also reminds me of when Larry and I raced up the steps of the Philadelphia Museum of Art, like Sylvester Stallone in *Rocky*. The incline was steep, I almost tripped, and my bunions hurt from wearing six-inch heels the night before. But the climb led to a worthwhile purpose—kicking Larry's butt!

You rarely know the big or small lessons you're learning when you're in the middle of them; you usually see them after the fact. I say better late than never. Some people spend their entire lives miserable and never realize those feelings were necessary in order for them to grow. I know it was easy for me to lose sight of God's purpose when I suffered from anxiety. Even after I realized that in a roundabout way, my scary condition could bring others peace—how's that for irony?—it took me five stubborn years to embrace my gift. But once I accepted that it was part of a bigger plan, I let myself learn all I could. This made me feel empowered, which helped me see that my past wasn't a waste. Instead of remembering this period as the twenty-five years that nearly ruined my life, I saw it as God's long-term investment in redirecting my path.

I used to get upset wondering how much better off I'd be if anxiety didn't "hold me back," but my take on that period of time has changed. Listen, I might not have met Larry at work or had kids young if I'd had a career in Manhattan, or been surrounded by friends and family when I accepted my gift, if I'd felt safe and secure moving away from them. Things worked out as they were supposed to as soon as I looked for healing and guidance, found it, and then ran with it. I welcomed my path and stayed open to my lessons, and I've been blessed ever since. In a lot of ways, anxiety's been one hell of a teacher.

Lessons + Purpose = A Chunky Scarf?

Life reminds me of one of those fancy knitting projects on Pinterest—your learned lessons and life events create intricate patterns, and the recurring stitch is your purpose. Whether you volunteer, make people laugh, or start political movements, you're meant to make a difference in some way. I realize that it's easy for me to say that Spirit wants us to live with intent, since they're in my ear all day, talking about how much there is to know. But hey, I'm not letting their words go unnoticed. You've got me, and I've got a big mouth! These lips have a purpose!

A lot like your lessons, your purpose doesn't have to be prestigious or put you in the spotlight. Who cares if you never become a celebrated novelist, brain surgeon, or the next Kardashian? Your purpose could mean a lot on a smaller scale. It might be about prioritizing family, improving your community, or caring for animals. There are a lot of cats out there that need foster homes!

So here's a question about lessons and purposes that comes up a lot these days: If your soul knows its purpose in Heaven, and you die in a public catastrophe, was that "fated" too? A lot of mediums believe that in the case of life-changing tragedies like 9/11, a devastating tsunami, or even a mass shooting, the deceased souls chose this specific type of death before coming to earth as part of their purpose. But Spirit's never told me this happens so expressly. I don't feel souls volunteer to become part of specific events, since stuff like terrorism, war, and gun violence occur because of free will (you could argue that the 2004 Thailand tsunami did too, thanks to global warming). What Spirit does tell me happens is that with, say, 9/11's first responders' souls, they knew they'd pass doing a civic duty, or with soldiers, that they'd die serving their country— all during a block of time called their "destiny." So when Spirit makes a cameo in well-known disasters, all their souls knew was that they'd (1) die within an allotted window while (2) pursuing lessons that impacted their soul growth and others on (3) their soul's generally charted path from God.

When you learn lessons, you don't suddenly get richer, become mayor, or turn into a Positive Polly. You gain something much harder to earn and more valuable—wisdom. Learning lessons isn't about being perfect, it's about recognizing that your time here unfolds the way it's meant to, as you make choices that fulfill you. This reminds me of a woman I read in Atlantic City, whose son suddenly died and donated almost all of his organs. As a result, his wife had his body cremated and kept his ashes. Too bad the guy's mom wanted to spread them in Aruba. Needless to say, Mom was still furious about this when I read her at my live show, so her son's soul had me insist, "I need you to love my family and children more than the anger you have for not spreading my cremains." Do you know, the lady still wouldn't let go of her frustration? I can only hope that Spirit somehow revisits this topic with her so she can heal, since I sensed that it's keeping her from feeling peace, finding happiness, and gaining useful wisdom. For now, it is what it is.

As you make your way through this book, consider the lessons Spirit's shared with me and place them in your life in a way that makes sense to you. Will I leave lessons out? Of course! I'm not God, and I'm not you. You're here to learn your own lessons, and not even a medium with very impressive nails can point you to what exactly your lessons are. You need to figure them out, but I'm happy to help where I can. Now pass me that snack already.

2

Everything Begins with Faith

I like to attend mass when I'm on tour, and while I'm there I ask God to guide me to guests at my live show who will benefit the most from Spirit's healing and validation. I also request that He give these people what they can handle that day to make things easier. So during a quick trip to Worcester, Massachusetts, Larry and I went to a parish called St. John's Catholic Church. There are a lot of churches in town, but I felt drawn to this one.

The service was wonderful, but what really spoke to me was the deacon's homily. In it, he read a well-known parable that says if you have faith the size of a mustard seed, everything is possible. Or, in his words, "If you have even the slightest bit of faith, then you have hope, and if you have hope, you have love." I couldn't stop thinking about this insightful tidbit, so I added the line to the speech I use to open my shows.

Later that day, toward the end of my event, Spirit guided me to the venue's side balcony to read a man whose wife died from a brain tumor. I thought he looked familiar but couldn't place him; I felt compelled to say I went to mass at St. John's that morning. Can you believe that the husband said he was their deacon and thought my faith, hope, love intro sounded familiar? Holy moly, what are the odds? Forget that I was busted for stealing the nice man's line. I don't think it's a coincidence that he and I were brought together! The guy got an amazing reading, and I saw his attendance as a sign from God that if a deacon's at my show, He appreciates my faith and thinks we could all use more of it.

The 411 on Faith

Faith feels like a perfect first lesson to talk about, because as the mustard seed parable teaches, everything we do, believe, achieve, and are is more powerful when it starts with faith. People think faith only has to do with religion, but it's more than that. From a spiritual standpoint, your faith can be related to God (which is what the deacon meant) or a higher power. But day to day, you might put faith in a partner for love, friends to make you smile, your court system to uphold the law, or a contractor to renovate your kitchen by Christmas.

A few areas where I place faith are in God for guidance, my team to pull off a good show, and my family to tolerate me when I'm acting bananas. You must also trust in yourself, like when I believe I can channel dead people who replace my thoughts and feelings with their own—talk about a leap of faith! Even if you're prone to doubt and cynicism verses hope and optimism, I'll bet you put faith in more than you think or admit. I've actually found that people who claim to have little or no faith want it most. Besides, if you don't have faith, what *do* you have? Heavy expectations for yourself and others, God forbid either let you down.

Spirit's taught me that the best outcomes occur when you release your fears and hesitations and move forward with faith. It shows Spirit that you trust their direction one hundred percent. This isn't easy to do—faith takes practice. But

> *Faith takes practice. But faith also begets faith. You gain faith by using it, watching it work, and even when it disappoints you.*

faith also begets faith. You gain faith by using it, watching it work, and even when it disappoints you. I feel faith is a force to be reckoned with. If you let it take the lead, it'll give you the hope to keep on. Say you lose your job but see it as a blessing in disguise. You'll feel motivated to look for a new one, and when you get the position because you act like a confident go-getter, you'll have *more* faith the next time you need it! This might be the Law of Attraction, Spirit looking out, or both, but I don't ask for much detail about how this works. I just have faith!

Finding Your Faith

Faith is also linked to your expectations, and it's hard to have positive ones when crummy things happen. Faith is tested when someone you love is sick, has died, or lets you down. When your plans go to hell, despite your heart's desire, it's normal to cling to faith or run from it. But if you can just hold on to your faith, it will help you see hard times as part of a journey and not a punishment. I've read so many people who know tragedy beyond anything I could imagine, and yet their faith is freakin' unshakable.

I don't know many people who've turned their back on faith or God entirely. They might get angry and need to work through some pain, but Spirit almost always brings them back home. It's like their intuition or God reminds them of where they need to be. When I was in Indianapolis, I read a couple named Melissa and Eric, who'd suffered a terrible miscarriage and health scare. On their way to the show, Melissa, who went to church every Sunday growing up, told Eric that she needed more trust and guidance in her life, and that she wanted to go back to church; Eric, whose mom never forced the God thing, still got it and agreed to join her. I found this out later, because when I read them, the first thing I asked was if they were religious, because Eric's mom's soul wanted them to know she was in the car with them when they were having their faith talk! She also told me they had good news, so Melissa let it slip that they were finally having a baby. I'd only just met them, but my heart jumped for joy! Eric's mom's soul added that despite any fears, the baby would be perfectly healthy and Eric would be a terrific dad.

After so much validation about their beliefs and future, the two now attend church together. As Melissa says, "I've found my faith again, and with it, a comfort and peace. It's been amazing to feel there's a greater good, accept that everything happens for a reason, and watch Eric stay open to the experience since he wasn't fully involved in the church before."

Faith is about showing up and starting from a place of yes. A hopeful, loving faith isn't an empty-headed wish either—it tends to come with an instinctual sense of knowing that what you believe will unfold. So where does that feeling come from? Spirit, namely God, your guides, and loved ones. And while I get a lot of info from Spirit, even I don't know how every situation will turn out. In serious matters like when Pop Brigandi died of a heart attack, and trivial ones like whether I'll win at Bingo, I work with the same faith that you guys do.

When the Going Gets Tough, Faith Gets You Going

Faith is about embracing the unknown, yet when I accepted my gift, God asked me to use it to help renew people's faith by offering "proof," so to speak, that there's more to life than what's in the physical world. Sounds counterintuitive, right? But if you believe in my abilities, I guess it gives you permission to have faith during other seemingly uncertain situations. I just love that every person who walks through my door exercises faith and leaves with a lot more of it.

So much of faith, then, is about trust. Trusting others and yourself. Trusting your journey, choices, and lessons. Believing there's a plan. Faith is also about going all-in and managing fear later. When you let worry take over, you think controlling a situation will make it happen, since you feel useful, capable, and safe. But faith asks you to feel OK about not being in control. Faith is asking for God's will and the highest good of all concerned. If you let go and trust your guidance—be it a higher power or your own instincts—faith will show up for you. Spirit works the same way. When you believe in their signs and symbols, they come more often, and I feel this happens because you've demonstrated faith.

It can be hard to know when to have faith but not act foolish.

When you want something so badly, you can block yourself from what's supposed to occur and spend time hoping for a moment that's not going to happen. Spirit says you'll know you're not spiritually intended to be in a situation when you feel you're at your wit's end; that's Spirit poking you to change direction. If you don't listen, you'll feel frustrated and negative, and your disappointment will affect everything and everyone you encounter. You'll lose faith and feel the opposite of hope and love.

During a live show in Durham, North Carolina, I read a couple named Jaime and Kris, who'd both lost a parent. Like Melissa and Eric earlier in this chapter, I knew they'd struggled with pregnancy and I felt a strong connection to a child; the big difference was that Spirit didn't show me that Jaime was knocked up! Good thing she said they were expecting through a surrogate—I thought I was losing it for a sec. Jaime's mom's soul then stepped forward to say that she knew they were cleaning and restoring some objects for the baby, which turned out to be an old rocking chair and bassinet that belonged to Jaime's mom. She also showed me a book with family photos, and Jamie said she'd written about their parents in a baby book the night before and talked about which photos to include.

But unlike Melissa and Eric, whose renewal of faith had to do with God, this reading was intended to renew Jaime's faith in herself and her family. Her mom's soul said Jaime feared she'd be a bad mom, so Spirit needed her to know she'd be great. This was so cool, because Kris later shared that Jaime was always afraid she'd fall short as a parent, to the degree that they debated having kids. The most touching news, though, was when her mom's soul said she personally guided their surrogate to them. There wasn't a dry eye in the theater! "Our message reminded us that love and faith are important and powerful forces," Kris told me later. "I also came away with a deeper belief in a higher power." There you have it.

You never know when faith will deliver your most heartfelt needs. At a live show in Ottawa, I read a woman named Sandra whose husband committed suicide fifteen years prior, and his soul couldn't wait to share the lessons he learned about love since crossing over. And while suicide is never part of your journey, his soul was at peace. Spirit has told me that during a suicide victim's life review, its soul has to come to terms with what an early exit means for growth—and that's what I loved so much about this reading. The man's soul proved that it's making progress by thanking his wife for loving him unconditionally. This was a big deal, because during their marriage he'd had multiple affairs, though she stayed with him and their three kids because she always loved him. After years of hoping her husband's soul was in a good place, Sandra felt an overwhelming calm to hear that at last, he gets what life is about. "Knowing that he's finally learning what love is, and how to love, gave me hope and renewed my belief in everlasting life with our Creator," she told me. When you have faith, everything is possible.

3

It Takes Patience to Learn Patience

The thought of writing about patience makes me impatient. I have a million things that needed to get done yesterday, and it's not in my nature to slow down! I'm sure patience is one of my major lessons, and let me tell you, it's a tall order. Because to have patience with yourself and others, you must also have compassion, kindness, nurturing, and understanding. Spirit says patience is an example of why it takes so long to master some of your lessons—this is one of those Big Kahuna lessons with smaller ones under it.

We all need patience to get through life. I could see where you might feel anxious to skip some of the lessons in this book, thinking, *Gratitude? Blame? I could take it or leave it.* You might not have a very contented life or soul if you do this, but . . . you'd get by. As for patience, you couldn't survive a day without tearing out your hair if you didn't have a grasp on this value. Four-way stops, airport security, bank lines, your dog trying to take a whiz in the snow—all these can test your patience and crawl under your skin.

You know what else takes patience? Learning lessons. Just sayin', it's worth getting under control.

I think our society's losing an increasing amount of patience every day, because related traits that you'd hope would be instinctual, like compassion and kindness, have gone by the wayside. We're overeager, impulsive, easily irritated, and always on edge. We don't like to live uncomfortably—take cell phones, for example. We expect a phone to also access email, play music, download movies, take pictures, and entertain us with a million apps. And when it has the gall to need an update that makes things go faster, but the update causes a glitch? We want to chuck it out the window! We need instant results, or else. Too bad Spirit says you have to let go to learn patience. Do they have a sense of humor or what?

Wait Now, Win Later

People don't know how to wait anymore, though there's a lot to gain from delayed gratification. Don't just take Spirit's word for it. Have you heard of the famous Stanford marshmallow experiment? In the late sixties and early seventies, a series of studies were done where kids had the choice between getting one small reward like a marshmallow, cookie, or pretzel stick if they took it right away, or two small rewards if the poor things waited until the person conducting the experiment left the room and came back a few minutes later. Each kid knew that if he or she rang a bell on the desk while the experimenter was gone, he'd come right back and the child could eat one marshmallow but not have a second. That's so hard for a little one! But years later, researchers actually found that the kids who delayed their gratification that day had fewer behavioral issues, did better on SATs, dealt well with stress, had longer attention spans, and had an easier time keeping friends later in life. Basically, the study shows that patience pays off, but I'm glad I wasn't chosen to be part of it. I'd have eaten the treats *and* asked for fondue on the side!

I'm not saying you should sit around waiting for The Good Life to walk up and give you a high five. Being patient doesn't mean feeling powerless, being a victim, tolerating bad situations, or taking someone else's bullshit either. You have free will and need to make choices that make your life meaningful. A lot of situations call for you to react or take matters into your own hands, but you need to know when to act and keep on it, and when to sit back and be patient. Most people don't know how to live with personalities or situations as they are, and feel the need to fix and fuss until everyone's ready to lose it. Sound familiar?

But guess what, kids. Spirit cares more about patience, and the compassion it takes to have it, than whether you had every right to make a stink about the slow barista at Starbucks or how your brother needs to hurry up and propose to his girlfriend. Choose tolerance instead. And as with faith, practicing patience helps you trust it to get you over hurdles. To be more patient, be more patient. Recognize when a situation is beyond your control, and change how you react to it. Accept and cope with things as they are, and learn to let go of how you want them to be.

Testing Your Patience

When you do have the ability to make change happen, Spirit likes to remind me that it doesn't need to occur overnight. Rome wasn't built in a day, and neither was your ability to deal with constant, thorny emotions. I'm thinking of sorrow, blame, and other complicated feelings that demand patience with yourself and everyone around you, because we make sense of difficulties at different paces.

To be patient, you have to be good to yourself and others. Grief, in particular, is a great example of an emotion whose healing relies on patience and self-kindness, since you have to tolerate the amount of time it takes to learn and absorb what you're being taught. If you're sad, you might cry five times today, but you know what? Maybe you'll cry only four times tomorrow. Slow and steady progress needs a lot of compassion, empathy, and nurturing to allow it to occur.

I always say I have the best clients and fans, but nobody has more patience than the people who attend my live shows. I know everyone hopes I'll read them, so they sit calmly and with faith that I'll reach them eventually. I might even start to read a person, then stop and come back at the end of the show. For two hours, I'm a walking test of your patience! This reminds me of a reading I did in Hamilton, Canada, for a woman named Candyse, whose daughter Taya died from a brain tumor at four and a half years old. Candyse came to my show on Taya's birthday, which was bittersweet for her. That morning, Candyse had brought cupcakes and coffee to the medical staff at the hospital and visited the cemetery. Her family released pink and purple balloons, and watched one of them float off on its own.

At the show, Candyse listened to me give other people closure and hoped it would soon be her turn. The clock ticked as she prayed that I'd connect with Taya's soul before the event was over. Just as Candyse was losing hope, I turned to her and said, "Is it your daughter's birthday today?" Candyse burst into tears. I took that as a "yes." Spirit mentioned the balloon release and the one that strayed from the bunch. I sensed the incredible bond Taya's soul has with her brother Tristan, and that she's with him when he does sports. Her soul also showed me he used to paint her nails and brush her hair (he'd even given her a spa day at home before her final trip to the hospital!), and then laughed at how her brother Kyc still plays with her dress-up shoes, which he'd done the week before, and said she's with him when he does this. Taya's soul gave her family what they needed most that day—to spend her birthday together—which made their wait worth all the agita.

So what are you waiting for? Give patience a chance. I'm a firm believer that patience brings healing to the mind, body, and soul. In fact, whenever I have ants in my pants, I substitute intolerance with gratitude, thanking God for His blessings—it's like the spiritual version of replacing sugar with Splenda. And when things don't go the way I'd hoped, I try to trust they'll get better instead of rushing to figure out how to do them my way. Listen, I don't think we're always going to act and react in the way that we're supposed to. But I think aiming for a calm soul is better than feeling huffy all the time, and that's as good a start as any.

> *Whenever I have ants in my pants, I substitute intolerance with gratitude, thanking God for His blessings—it's like the spiritual version of replacing sugar with Splenda.*

4

Laughter Is No Joke

I love to laugh, whether it's because my family is making fun of each other or I'm cracking myself up with a corny joke. Spirit says your sense of humor plays an ample role in good health, a strong soul, feeling centered, and battling the blues, so I try to keep my funny bone sharp. Let's also remember that laughter literally feels good. It almost immediately changes your perspective, lifts your mood, and distracts you in the very best way. Like, look what happens when I do this:

What did the ocean say to the sand? Nothing—it just waved!
Come on, that's a good one. OK, what about now:
Why don't skeletons go to scary movies? They don't have the guts!
Stop it! And what if I said . . .
How does Moses make his tea? Hebrews it.

All right, that's just freakin' hysterical. You might not agree that I'm ready to headline at the Comedy Cellar, but you have to admit that your heart feels lighter than it did before you started this chapter. Just imagine how you'd feel if you made *your* kind of humor a priority every day. Laughter would have such an uplifting effect that you'd be making all kinds of funnies in no time.

When I channel, I ask Spirit to communicate with humor, personality, and happiness; I feel it's the best way to hear from someone you miss, especially if the person was funny in the physical world, because then it's a validation too. You also spend enough time feeling down about a loved one's death that if I can make you feel like you're with them in a positive way, I will. Spirit also ups their humor by making me talk or act certain ways, or giving me crazy validations, so even if they were miserable at the end of life, you can hold on to this memory.

I get a kick out of channeling a soul who was a real pisser in the physical world, because Spirit makes me feel like I'm the most hilarious person in the room. You know when you're telling a story at the dinner table, and everyone's laughing, and you're on top of the world? It's a high that runs through your whole body. That's how Spirit makes me feel before I say a word. I feel like I'm already being funny before I'm actually funny, if that makes sense. Then I go with it. For example, once I channeled the soul of a gentleman's daughter, singing and dancing up a storm. It felt like she was standing next to me, so I began speaking to her, laughing and gesturing as if she were right there, even if only I sensed her (listen, at least Clint Eastwood had a chair—I just had my zebra rug). Spirit said, "Tell my dad I'm dancing on stage!" So here I am, describing her moves like, *Look at her go!* I looked nuts, but her dad said, "That's exactly what my daughter did. She was so entertaining—she loved to dance and sing on stage!"

When Spirit Thinks They're a Comedy Troupe

Some people don't like that I channel with laughter, because nothing about death is supposed to be funny. Says who? Yes, I'm communicating, sensing, and feeling souls that have departed, but just because you're in mourning doesn't mean you have to stop living. There's nothing disrespectful or careless about taking a second out of your day to smile for a change. We tend to get so caught up in our grief that we forget how to have fun. But Spirit wants you to at least try. They'll say to a person stuck in the darkest, loneliest place, "I give you permission to laugh," or "I want you to make a conscious decision that the next time you leave the house, you'll laugh at life. When you get home, then you can grieve my loss."

> *Just because you're in mourning doesn't mean you have to stop living. There's nothing disrespectful or careless about taking a second out of your day to smile for a change.*

Granting permission is also Spirit's way of teaching you that you can *choose* to laugh, if you give yourself a good enough reason. Today, your reason is their consent or request; gradually, you'll find your own motivations. Laughing also helps you exist in the moment, so you don't dwell on the past or wait for future sadness to strike. Now let me ask you a serious question:

How did the tree get on the Internet? It logged in!

You didn't expect that right? But you're laughing, maybe a little? Man, I'm on a roll today! So where was I—oh yeah, Spirit and laughter.

Because Spirit knows how much a good chuckle can lighten your soul, they like to encourage other souls to channel with humor too if their energy isn't flowing as easily. At one of my live shows, I read three moms who didn't know each other but were seated in the same area a couple of rows apart. Often Spirit places people near each other if their loved ones' souls share a similar type of death or message—this makes it easier for them to piggyback. One of the women had a young son who'd recently died, and the other two had lost their daughters, seventeen and eighteen years old, prior to that. The seventeen-year-old starts channeling like gangbusters, so we're teasing her, calling her "a real Spirit hog." The other girl's soul was like, "I've got nothing left to say! She's stealing all my messages!" Frick and Frack, those two.

Meanwhile, the boy's mom wasn't as far along in her healing process as the other mothers, and his soul was nervous about stepping forward. He knew she was still in a fragile state and didn't want to spook or upset her. So you'll never guess what these two girls' souls did—they began cheering his soul on! Then the seventeen-year-old made *me* do a cheer, and here I am, busting into a sis-boom-ba in my crystal heels. At that point, the girl's mom turns to me and goes, "That would be my daughter! She always cheered for teammates on her varsity soccer team and was also a cheerleader!" Can you believe it? The girls gave his soul a boost of encouragement and taught by example. All the moms smiled ear to ear.

Come on Spirit, Let the Good Times Roll

If a person has a hard time remembering lighter memories, Spirit likes to suggest making a Memory Jar. Not only does this activity put your mind and soul in a contented place, it teaches you to get resourceful about making yourself feel good. For this project, you take an old jar, like a mayonnaise or bell jar, and leave it by the front door with a pen and notepad next to it. Every time someone comes or goes, he or she has to write down a funny memory, thought, or emotion about the person who died. If you have five memories, use five pieces of paper. Maybe your partner liked to sing "We Will Rock You" in his pjs, or your mom dressed like Wilma from *The Flintstones* every Halloween. Whatever made the happy tears roll and your belly hurt so good, put it in the jar. Then, when you need to smile, you can pull out a memory to read and remember! FYI, Spirit is so big on not taking things for granted that there's a second lesson here: feeling gratitude for a support system that celebrates the departed with so much love. I should also say—

What's the best way to defend yourself against a gang of carnival clowns? Go for the juggler!

Get it? Like "jugular" . . . ? All right, all right. I'll get back to the lessons.

Spirit shows me that laughter is spiritually beneficial, because your vibration increases when you laugh. Also, the more positive your energy is, the easier it is to learn lessons. I've noticed that when I read a happy person, the soul feels lighter and higher than a person who's depressed; being empathic, I can sense and feel when this kind of

Laughter is spiritually beneficial, because your vibration increases when you laugh. Also, the more positive your energy is, the easier it is to learn lessons.

thing happens. It's also simpler for me to get information from higher vibrations, not to mention more pleasant. Listen, I'm the one who's talking to dead people—I like it when they're in a good mood!

Spirit says laughter is effective medicine for the soul, because it mends you in a deep way. If I'm giving a person advice from Spirit, and it actually begins their healing process in that moment, I can feel the person's soul lighten up. I'm not surprised that laughter's health benefits are one area that Spirit and science are in agreement. Plenty of studies show that laughter has healing properties—it reduces anger and stress, boosts endorphins, relieves pain, increases immunity, relaxes muscles, and can help some heart and lung conditions. When you laugh, it feels cleansing, you know? Your soul is like a self-cleaning oven that way.

Laugh, and the Universe Laughs with You

Laughter is more contagious than the common cold. Whether you let out a giggle or double over with good tears, the moment connects you with everyone else who's enjoying it too. One time, I read a couple in Indiana who'd lost their son. His soul was doing a terrific job validating that he was at peace, but apparently as I channeled, his mother kept asking him in her head if he was with her sister in Heaven. So out of nowhere, I felt the need to say, "Do you remember that old Big Mac commercial? 'Two all beef patties, special sauce, lettuce, cheese, pickles, onions, on a sesame seed bun?'" I kept hearing the jingle and seeing a T-shirt with a Big Mac on it. Sure enough, the woman and her sister used to spend hours memorizing and singing that song! It's been decades since that commercial aired, and I was flipping out that Spirit helped me get it right! More importantly, this validated that the woman's son was with her sister, as she had hoped and wanted to know. The audience was also hysterical laughing, and I guarantee that the grumpiest among them drove home singing that ridiculous commercial in the car.

In my world everyone laughs, dead and alive. My team, friends, family, and Spirit—we laugh hard, laugh easily, and have a similar sense of humor. Except maybe Larry, who's more of an inside laugher and gets a kick out of The Three Stooges, which I don't get at all. But I'll keep at him. I think he might like this one:

A dyslexic man walked into a bra . . .

That's good stuff, right?

5

Just Do You

I eat too many carbs, I can't dance for shit, and I pollute the air with my hairspray. But I also recycle the spray cans, make a good meatball, remember birthdays, and am always there for my kids. I'm imperfect in so many ways, but listen, I am who I am. Take it or leave it, no apologies. The day I got honest about this, which was a major step toward honoring my soul, every part of my life got better.

When I talk about authenticity, I don't want to sound like an Oprah wannabe. She practically owns the idea of being your best self, and I feel no need to trump or compete with that. But I would like to share what Spirit says about this topic and how I learned to discover who I am, so that it might help you. Unlike O, I don't have a team of experts on hand, but I do have an incredible "advisory board"—God and Spirit. And they don't even ask for insurance benefits!

Go Gaga Over Yourself

If I said, "Being authentic means being yourself," you might think, *Duh lady, who else am I gonna be?* But you have more options than you realize. You play a lot of roles throughout your life and each comes with expectations. You might wear the hat of a CEO, PTA president, devoted wife, or stepfather, but let me ask you, who is the person behind those titles and what traits epitomize the real you? If your employees, peers, or family didn't label you, who would you be?

You came into this world with authenticity, in that nobody else is you. Spirit says your truest values and gifts live in your soul, which is its most pure when you're born. And if you look at who you were as a child, that's probably the last time you were closest to your true self, since negative factors like doubt and judgment hadn't affected you yet. Whenever I see a little girl wearing a poncho and two different socks, or a boy picking a dandelion for his mom, I'm amazed at how unique, sincere, and trusting their natures are. Wouldn't it be great to feel that way again?

Spirit's lessons about authenticity make me think of Lady Gaga's song "Born This Way," especially when she sings, *Don't hide yourself in regret / Just love yourself and you're set*, because her advice is so dead-on. The real key to pulling off this one-two punch, though, is what Gaga sings in Italian: *mi amore vole fe yah*, which means "Love needs faith." When I heard that line, it made me so giddy to know she truly gets it on both a worldly and soul level. Sending her all the sfogliatelle in Italy couldn't have demonstrated my gratitude! It takes faith to love who you are, despite where you've been. On a related note, Spirit says that love is the basis of your journey and lessons here, because God is unconditional love, so you have to know how to

> *Love is the basis of your journey and lessons here, because God is unconditional love.*

love yourself to be the soul He wants you to be for others too.

Becoming authentic affects you in every way—spiritually, emotionally, and physically. If you're not real on the inside, the rest of your life gives you away. You might wrestle with faith, stay in a bad relationship, suffer from anxiety, sink into a depression, or have weight issues or pain fed by inner demons. It wasn't smooth sailing when I learned about my abilities, but as I took baby steps toward accepting them, I felt my life fall into place and make sense. Spirit led me to learn how to embrace my gift and religious beliefs, trust friends who didn't think I was cuckoo, and use mediumship to help others. Because I had faith, love, and was committed to my journey, I gradually saw that I didn't need to hide my soul, even if others raised an eyebrow. Even now, I never ask anyone to believe in what I do. It doesn't matter, because I believe in it.

Make no mistake—authenticity isn't about just accepting who and where you are; it's also about discovering and then embracing your best self with everything you have. You might even create it from scratch! I always like to suggest soul-searching to help you figure out your path. For me, this process included daily meditation and prayer, where I had hard conversations with God and my guides about who I was and what I wanted from life. I told them that if my soul was meant to connect with those who've crossed over, I'd accept this gift, but I only wanted to know good things. I also wanted to use my gift to help others. I asked for people to be placed in my path to help me grow and thanked God for sending me invaluable support, like my parents and husband. Finally, I did the hands-on work of honing and understanding the breadth of my abilities. Spirit wants you to embark on your own discovery, but instead of understanding the Other Side, take a class or open a charter school for children with autism—whatever speaks to you. Ultimately, soul-searching teaches you how to let your instincts guide you to choices that align with your best self.

Soul-searching is the hardest thing I've ever done in my life, because you have to look deep within your essence, evaluate where you are on your path, think about the lessons you're being taught, and explore who you're meant to be. During this time, you might also realize that the qualities people tell you are flaws might just be God-given attributes. Believe it or not, I've been called a mild pain in the ass before, but I feel this is just another way of saying I don't settle. That trait comes in handy, whether I'm buying apples or standing up for my abilities.

When you're not actively soul-searching, get in the daily habit of listening to what your inner voice has to say. You'll know it's the direction of God, guides, or your angels when it offers guidance and doesn't tell you exactly what to do. The more in touch you are with your intuition, the louder and more exact it becomes. This might sound silly, but you can also try carrying on a conversation with your gut, to see if it talks back. In your head, ask it to point you toward a new job, the right doctor, or what you should say to your teenager who's always late for her curfew. The answers will sound very faint and in your own voice, because Spirit speaks through your thoughts; it's like when a song is stuck in your head, and you mentally sing it all day. You can "hear" it, but you're also singing it in the back of your mind. You understand that? Spirit's advice will get more precise as you practice, because you're learning to listen and be open to change.

Be *Your* Best, Not Someone Else's

Now, I don't want to hear that after weeks of intense soul-searching, Spirit or your intuition told you that your big lesson involves quitting your job, moving to Maui, working on your tan, and drinking piña coladas all day on the beach. I don't know, maybe it could. Perhaps your lessons are about learning to relax or go with the flow . . . but I'd have a hard time believing it, since authenticity involves being the most excellent version of you, not the laziest. It's also tough to listen carefully to your soul when you're drunk on rum. So, nice try.

I've always told my kids that I'd support any career they wanted to have, as long as they did their best at it; I want them, the way Spirit wants you, to live an authentic life while using their gifts. Like with Victoria, I've said, "You want to be a dog walker? Go ahead. But you're going to be the best damn dog walker you can be." I'd want her to be the dog walker who's in it because she loves animals and her soul likes to care for others. The kind of thoughtful, genuine person that instinctively brings your pet hiking or to the beach, teaches her tricks, organizes playdates with other dogs, and rolls around in the grass with her on sunny days.

Spirit says being your best benefits you now and in the after-life. Most immediately, don't you want to go through life happy instead of miserable or half-invested? I thought so. You might think I'm oversimplifying things, but does everything have to be complicated? It doesn't. Also, spending your day doing an activity that's "so you" can profoundly nourish your soul, since feeling fulfilled raises your vibration and makes you more receptive to learning lessons.

As you become more authentic, you won't only realize what makes you thrive; you will also see, almost immediately (because it becomes instinctual), what brings you down. And you'll begin to appreciate what makes you special. Years ago, my great-grandparents on my mom's side ran a family restaurant in Brooklyn called Julie's. It was the most authentic manifestation of who these two were—they loved cooking, eating, and serving others, they enjoyed working beside family and meeting new people, and they valued a hard day at the "office." But what I loved more than their original Neopolitan pizza is that my great-grandparents were their best when using their gifts. That made them impressive.

When you start pursuing authenticity, Spirit says you have to be careful to not let the process consume you so much that other areas of your life suffer. I've learned that too much of a good thing is bad, even if it makes you excited or helps others. I think I have the most fascinating and valuable job, but I can be short-fused and worthless when I let work run my life (and then there goes my lesson in patience, on top of it all). You can't honor your soul when you're not balanced, and I get out of whack when I stress about juggling a tour, live shows, writing and promoting a book, shooting episodes, and seeing longtime clients for their private readings. The thing is,

I'm not busier than most of you are—my schedule's no more full, say, than a mom's who plans her life around a husband, kids, a job, pets, and possibly caring for elderly parents. Crazy is crazy. But as soon as you realize that you're no longer your best to you or others, you need to slow that train down. Your new self-awareness should help you notice if this is an issue.

Own Who You Are

Other people can make or do something that pleases you, like buy you a potted orchid or get your car washed without asking (hint, hint Little Larry), but you're responsible for your soul's joy and everyone it touches. This includes when a loved one's soul tells me that a living person "feels different" or doesn't fit in at school, and in most of these cases, Spirit doles out tough love. I'll say, "Bullies have issues and want you to feel as miserable as they do. But they're not strong enough to make you do anything. Who cares what one person thinks? People can be cruel, screw 'em. You have a lot to offer. Don't let others hold you back."

Believe me, I can relate to people who feel like outsiders and are always being judged; a big part of my initial growth was not letting every skeptic and naysayer bring me down. If I did, do you think I'd be where I am today? But authenticity doesn't mean that you or your life has to be or seem perfect either.

> *Authenticity doesn't mean that you or your life has to be or seem perfect either. You wouldn't want a flawless experience—you'd have nothing to push against, no reason or chance to grow.*

You wouldn't want a flawless experience—you'd have nothing to push against, no reason or chance to grow. Once you're on a path to self-discovery and authenticity, you'll see how conflicts are in your way for a reason.

Spirit says the relationship between authenticity and the soul is always evolving. This is great to know, because if such a partnership were only left to your head, the opposite might happen. Most people let fear and the need to please get in the way of being themselves. You try to be who you think others want you to be, or who you think you should be—not who you are. When I talk about my gift, I always say I'm becoming better at using it every day. I'm never going to be like, *Hey everyone, I know everything about Heaven and Spirit!* People always ask why I act so surprised when I hear from Spirit, and it's because no matter how much I channel, they always teach me something new.

You know the old saying "You can't take it with you?" One of the most genuine souls I've channeled taught me that this phrase does not apply to authenticity. At a show in Indiana, I read a gorgeous woman who'd hoped to hear from her daughter. She did, but what she never expected was that the daughter's soul would bring the woman's ex-husband with her! The minute I said his soul was there, she laughed, pointed at the ceiling, and warned, "Now you behave, George!" I sensed that she didn't want him to give away dirty secrets or get fresh with me! His fiery energy reminded me of the subway soul in *Ghost*, played by the late Vincent Schiavelli, who breaks open the cigarette machine because he wants a smoke (and in real life, died from lung cancer).

Interestingly, I could feel George's soul rein it in at this woman's request, as it thanked her for how she paid her respects to him at the end. I said to the woman, "Why do I feel like you didn't go to a public viewing?" She explained that as The Ex, she didn't want to be at the funeral home during regular viewing hours, so she asked a guy who worked there to sneak her in later. George got a kick out of her shrewdness! As his soul grew on the Other Side, it never lost its feisty, authentic edge—take it or leave it, no apologies.

6

Nobody Wins the Blame Game

Blame is one of the more challenging lessons that Spirit talks about when I channel. It's a complicated topic, mostly because Spirit's reactions are different depending on whether the criticism is turned inward or directed at others. And it's hard enough for us in the physical world to get why people point fingers, so you can only imagine the many angles Spirit uses to teach this subject.

Just think about all the ways that blame plays out in real life. It can be a feeling or an action. It can be a knee-jerk comeback or thought-out response. It might be the result of profound sorrow or nasty aggression. The damage blame causes can resolve quickly or take years to repair. It might ruin your life or hurt countless others who cross your path. It can keep you stuck in the past or be your worst coping mechanism as you bulldoze ahead. It can be all of these things, or just some, in any combination, based on your experiences and how evolved your soul is in other areas, like forgiveness, patience, and staying positive. Yet no matter what,

Spirit insists this is one of the most important lessons you can learn.

In blame-worthy situations, Spirit objects to the negativity that anchors you to stagnant energy and keeps you from healing and learning lessons. Even at its most innocent, blame is never healthy. And just so you understand, the concept of blame has always seemed so pessimistic to me that I never gave it much thought before Spirit forced me to. So a lot of what I feel about blame that you're going to read in this chapter actually comes from Spirit's reactions to my readings. Spirit always shares my brain, but now I guess we also share an opinion on this topic!

Shouldering the Blame? Fuggedaboutit!

Spirit is mostly compassionate toward clients who blame themselves for their misfortunes. Maybe this is because people who carry blame for hard or confusing situations tend to do so when they struggle with faith, and Spirit sees no need to add insult to injury here. They know that it's difficult to accept that there's a reason for most tragic events. You also might wonder if you're responsible for the situation, especially when there seems to be no logical reason for what occurred.

It would be nice if life always offered us a cause and effect, but it doesn't work that way. So if you see the effect, like a hardship or death, but the cause feels random, as with a freak accident, it throws you. What's worse is if you think the effect could have been changed, as when a person dies from a seemingly preventable illness. The consequence is that self-blamers feel helpless and devastated, so they wedge themselves into the story to try to make sense of it.

If you unnecessarily blame yourself for an event, Spirit's first priority is to name one or more specific grounds for why you shouldn't carry this burden. They have me do this until I sense that your soul is calm enough to start healing. So Spirit might show me that a soul chose a death that would be quickest for you to heal from, ask me to insist that the soul's destiny was set, tell me the person died a certain way to help you learn a lesson or help others—or any mix of these positive and encouraging efforts.

These facts help clients in their own ways, but if you pull back from the individual stories, Spirit's overarching lesson is that you can't stop looking for reasons to heal. Also, these messages reinforce that some things are out of your hands once you're in this world, because your soul chose your journey and knew your destiny all along. Everything is part of a purpose, path, and lessons. So the next time you're tempted to take on blame, ask Spirit to help you figure out what you're being taught. At the very least, it will refocus your thoughts and stop the loop of regret.

While endlessly chiding yourself can cause you to feel lonely, what makes it worse is that self-blame rarely exists on its own. It's usually joined by guilt and anger, and the combination affects the loved ones around you, even if you think it's just your burden to carry. During a live show in Michigan, I read a terrific woman named Stephanie and her husband, Chad; Stephanie's brother Michael died from a heart attack at thirty-five years old. Right away, Michael's soul insisted I tell Chad, "Today, I'm going to give you back your wife." Stephanie always blamed herself for a lot of factors related to her brother's passing. In fact, his soul said Chad prayed to him every night, asking for the strength to care for Stephanie and her grieving mom, Phyllis; Chad said that was so true. What a good husband he is.

Spirit then explained three situations where blame weighed on Stephanie, and Michael's soul got to work alleviating it. First, as a registered nurse, Stephanie blamed herself for not realizing Michael wasn't taking good care of his health, which was breaking Chad's heart. To address this, Michael insisted his destiny was set (when Spirit tells me this, they're referring to a window of time in which our souls have chosen to leave this plane; so if Michael didn't have a heart attack that day, he might have been, say, hit by a bus three days later). Next, his soul showed me Stephanie was upset that she couldn't perform CPR on his body, which Stephanie said was the case: "No one would try as hard as I would to save him." Here, Spirit had me explain that her anger was useless, since Michael's soul had left his body by the time she arrived. Finally, Stephanie blamed herself for contributing to an issue with the funeral arrangements, but Michael's soul let her know that he was content with the decisions she made. He was funny about it, actually. His soul had me shout, "Fuggedaboutit!"—one of his favorite sayings.

As I passed on these reassuring messages from Spirit, Chad gave his wife gentle hugs and kisses; it was a touching moment for everyone. The couple received the support and clarity they needed, and the message quieted the side effects of blame. Stephanie specifically said, "Michael's messages calmed my grief, made me a little stronger, and helped me accept the things I cannot change."

You Think It's Everyone Else's Fault. How 'Bout It's Yours?

On the other side of the coin, Spirit has a pretty impatient attitude toward you blaming others, and man, so do I. God don't like ugly, and blame is one of the ugliest feelings you can push on another person. Insisting other individuals or factors are wrong or at fault, when you don't want to see them for what they are, react with empathy, or be held accountable, is a terrible way to handle an ordeal.

I realize that when you're grasping for answers, blame is a fast route to easy explanations, but it also leads to naive rationalizations that slow down your soul's growth. Your child was in a sledding accident? It's his babysitter's fault for letting him play in the snow! You never saved for retirement? It's your spouse's fault for not making you! Come on, are you kidding me with this? Blame just lets you escape reality and ignore the truth, especially when it's hard to swallow.

When I meet blamers, their general attitude seems to be that every problem out there is someone else's fault. But how can everyone in the world be messed up but them? Take my girlfriend Laura, who's had multiple treatments for severe Crohn's disease and related issues. The condition has caused obstructions, ulcers, fertility problems—you name it. But despite the fact that she was born with this disease, her mother won't stop blaming, blaming, blaming. She blames her daughter for having an imperfect diet, her surgeon for not "curing" her, God for "denying" her grand-children. . . .

These kinds of accusations are such a selfish reaction to a person's heartbreak, and you can see how her mother misfires negative energy at everyone around her. But like most classic blamers, I think she feels that if she had somewhere to direct her anger, she could stop searching for a "cause" and finally move on with her life. What Spirit would prefer is for Laura's mother to look for a valid but more enlightened reason for her daughter's ordeal. Maybe Laura was meant to learn tolerance, adopt a child, or here's an idea—teach her mother a lesson about blame! But because this requires soul-searching, would take longer, and may lead to a painful acceptance, Mom has sidestepped the lesson so far. Besides, blame seems to offer an answer where there isn't one, even if it never leads to the truth, which is why she keeps coming up with angry accusations.

To be clear, when I talk about blamers, I'm not referring to those who assign responsibility to what causes a situation to happen—like crediting a car accident to a drunk driver or hearing a judge find a man guilty of murder. Spirit appreciates knowledge, closure, and justice. The blame I mean is fueled by toxic emotions and angry words. It also has a sleazy relationship with guilt. When you internalize blame, you can become consumed by sorrow and guilt. But when you blame others, you lay the guilt on nice and thick to make yourself feel better, take the moral high ground, and make others feel bad about their choices. When you push off blame, you think you're smarter, and if you can get others on your side, you live for the validation. Too bad Spirit calls it like it is—a cruel waste of time.

Spirit's take on all blame is that it adds no value to your life and soul. It doesn't need to be mean to not serve a purpose either; senseless finger-pointing comes up a lot with loved ones of suicide victims who feel what I call "would-have-could-have-should-have-if-only's." They think, *If only I'd answered his call; his wife could have listened better; her son should have seen the signs.* When addressing these, Spirit will have me say, "Blame whoever you want, but that won't help you heal." They don't dwell on energy and emotions that go nowhere.

Say Your Apologies, Find the Good, and Get On with It

As you can see, Spirit feels there are better uses of your time than exercising blame. Spend it making yourself more patient with a situation, so if you need an answer, you can find it. Utilize it to be introspective, so you can learn a lesson and grow your soul. Even if you're not "at fault," take responsibility for what you did to contribute to the scenario and work it out if you can. Basically, use your energy to address a situation and move forward, without being defensive or slinging blame. You can make every excuse in the world, but how will you make things better?

And if you're even partially liable for a situation where blame's been tossed around, for the love of Spirit, own it. I recently got into a shouting match with a friend, and when it ended, I apologized for the way I acted. I took responsibility for the

> *Address a situation and move forward, without being defensive or slinging blame. You can make every excuse in the world, but how will you make things better?*

conversation getting out of hand, and I didn't blame the person, even though he said something to set me off. I did, however, feel bad for letting myself react in a terrible way, so that's what I apologized for. I smoothed things over without accepting that the fight was my fault and took responsibility for my words. Like those women always do on *The Real Housewives*, I did not say that I was sorry for my feelings, since your feelings are never wrong.

However, Spirit does say that your problems are your own, now and in Heaven. If you don't learn about blame and responsibility in this world, you'll relive blame-worthy experiences through the eyes of those who suffered from your crappy behavior or relearn it in the afterlife or another incarnation. This is why I'll never forget the reading we aired on *Long Island Medium* about a man who followed through with a difficult lesson he chose in his soul state—to carry the blame for his son's death and learn to work through the fallout, so his wife didn't have to. You've heard of manning up? This guy soul-ed up. Big time.

Here I read a couple named John and Sue, whose son, Shane, drowned in their pool while John was at home with him; Shane had Down syndrome and was four and a half years old when he passed. Usually, both parents watched him at all times and installed multiple safeguards to keep Shane safe, in case he slipped past their view. Yet when Sue left Shane with John to take their daughter to a party, a number of mishaps occurred. John took a call in another room and didn't reinforce the locked doors after working outside, he left the ladder down to their aboveground pool, which made it accessible, and he shut off the alarm system because the batteries were dying and he'd planned to replace them. This is how Shane wandered outside without his father knowing. When John got off the phone and checked on Shane, he found the back door open and Shane unconscious in the pool. John immediately called 911 and tried to resuscitate his son, but after being rushed to the hospital and lingering for two days, Shane was pronounced dead.

Sue was deeply angry at John and blamed him for her son's death. When I channeled Shane's soul, one of the first things he said was, "Please remind my mom that I tested her every day." Shane showed me that when he and his mother were alone together, he frequently tried to run outside alone too. His soul also showed me him pulling the door open and laughing—Shane knew he wasn't supposed to go by that pool. Sue confirmed that yes, her son loved being outside, so he always tried to open the doors and couldn't wait for the pool to be finished when it was being installed. "It was very typical of Shane to do this sort of thing," she later said. "It was his personality to go without asking. If he wanted something, he just did it."

Next came the reading's game-changer. Shane's spirit had me tell his father, "Your soul's journey was to carry this guilt for your wife." At this point, I was crying my eyes out because the message was so selfless and powerful, but I also could feel John's guilt empathically, and the heaviness was unreal. I turned to Sue and said, "You don't want to feel an ounce of what this man carries every day of his life." Shane's soul then said to me, "Theresa, my mom knows deep in her soul that it's not my dad's fault. Please tell them to take care of each other."

Sue touched her husband's hand during the reading, but did it help her understand their souls' shared lesson about blame? I'd hoped so, though I realize this is a difficult message to accept. Months after the show aired, Sue said she was still quite upset with John but has learned to put herself in his position and can't imagine how he gets through a day with his guilt. She's learning to forgive, have compassion, and finally see there were more reasons for her son's death than what her husband did and didn't do.

"We're working on our marriage, and trying to keep this family together, because that was Shane's message," she said.

One of the most liberating truths that Spirit shares with me is this: Whether you're carrying blame or throwing it in someone's face, you're exactly where you're supposed to be, even if that place is painful or one of searching or longing. So take responsibility and attempt to look at things differently. Try to discover the real answers and be compassionate. And if you're confused about who's to blame, move past that negative frame of mind. There's always a reason, if you take a minute to search for it.

> *Whether you're carrying blame or throwing it in someone's face, you're exactly where you're supposed to be, even if that place is painful or one of searching or longing.*

7

Roll with Acceptance

I have a plaque hanging in my kitchen that gets me going each day. I read it every morning as I make my protein shake, while secretly wishing I were eating pancakes for breakfast instead. On the sign are four lines of what's called "The Serenity Prayer," and though this meditation has been adopted by a number of twelve-step programs, you don't have to be in one to feel inspired by it:

> *God grant me the serenity*
> *To accept the things I cannot change;*
> *The courage to change the things I can;*
> *And the wisdom to know the difference.*

So simple, yet so brilliant! Even though acceptance is only mentioned in the first line, it speaks to me most. I use the prayer as a daily reminder to make acceptance the foundation of my day and the basis of everything I do and say.

Begin with Acceptance

I suspect that most people believe acceptance is where you go after all is lost; they think it's the same as defeat or resignation. Acceptance is even the fifth and last stage of grief, according to the famous Kübler-Ross model—the point you get to after battling denial, anger, bargaining, and depression. People think acceptance is where you end up when you're ready to let go, but that sounds more like surrender; in fact, Spirit shows me surrender happens when you feel defeated, beaten, and aware that it's time to move on. It's when you throw up your hands and admit you're in over your head or ready to try another way. But acceptance? That takes more initiative, and guts.

I use the word "acceptance" because, to me, accepting something is a positive way to begin and sustain an effort, not where you land once you're done trying. I think it takes a lot of trying to welcome, then use, acceptance in your life. If any of you readers are fancy linguists, please don't tell me I don't understand what the word "acceptance" means, based on its Old French origins or whatever. Nobody thinks I'm moonlighting as a college professor. I also realize that my intuition isn't Harvard freakin' University, but my soul has proven to be clever in its own ways.

In my frame of reference, acceptance has a few meanings. It's the act of receiving, as with a gift or apology—and spiritually, I see it as welcoming where you are on your soul's path, from Spirit who guide it. Acceptance is also about fitting in, as with social acceptance, or in your case, how you embrace the friends, lessons, and choices that fit into your purpose. Finally, acceptance is the act of believing something is true. It's part of believing in what Spirit has to teach you.

Similar to faith, acceptance teaches you to welcome the happy moments *and* the obstacles that upset and challenge you, because both teach you lessons. I know "The Serenity Prayer" says to "accept the things you cannot change," but I'm tempted to edit it on my sign with a red marker to say, "accept the things you can *and* cannot change." It would lose its meter, but I can accept that.

Because acceptance is about appreciating things as they are, this perspective lets you stay in the moment, value what's happening, and feel calm in your body, mind, and soul because you know Spirit is guiding your path. When you wake up in the morning, you never know what's going to happen, correct? You might get a tragedy, you might get a miracle. When you have acceptance, you realize everything is uncertain and simply receive what comes to you, because you also know it will be OK when you have faith in God's will.

When I read a person who's struggling with how a loved one passed, Spirit might have me point out, "Do we have to focus on how I died? You need to let go of that so you can heal from my loss. Because no matter what, I died. Would it be better if I died from a different cause? No, I'd still be dead, and you'd still be sad." Spirit likes to boil things down to their most basic, simple truths—here, that the person is no longer in this world—to help you reach acceptance, which in this example means healing from loss. Souls don't say, "Take your time making yourself nuts over how I died, and then start to heal." Right? They basically say, "How I died? It is what it is. Please accept that, or you'll never feel better."

The same way that Spirit says focusing on painful details can hold you back from healing, negative overthinking in your everyday life can distract you from recognizing and accepting your lessons, purpose, and path with faith and conviction. I'm not saying that the minute you hear about a disaster, you should be like, "Que sera sera!" You also shouldn't shut off your brain and stop making informed decisions. But when you fight acceptance with thoughts that become pessimistic and convoluted, it works against you. Spirit tells me that negative feelings and actions are complicated, but the truth is always simple.

> *Negative feelings and actions are complicated, but the truth is always simple.*

Acceptance Is Hard, and It Isn't Just About You!

Acceptance might not come so easy at first. For me, it requires consistent prayer, meditation, remembering to be grateful for my blessings, and asking Spirit for the highest good of all concerned. When you're regularly meditating or soul-searching, acceptance arrives more easily; taking time to connect with God and Spirit implies that you trust them to steer and protect you on your journey.

Whether I'm talking to your mother's soul or giving real-world advice to my nieces and nephews, I never question my words, because I believe everything I say and do is guided. Not because I'm the Long Island Medium, but because I accept what God and Spirit literally show me, and you can too. Seriously, let's all consider this for a minute: I manage to communicate with God, saints, angels, dead celebrities, and your deceased family and friends on a regular basis. I think it's pretty safe to say that the universe has demonstrated that it's so much bigger, more powerful, and more in control than any of us might have imagined!

Over the years, I've worked really hard at accepting life as it unfolds. It's been one tough lesson, but I think I'm getting better at it. Acceptance is appreciating who and where you are in this moment, warts and all, especially as you're growing. Spirit says this also leads to new possibilities, since acceptance helps you see your life for what it is. If you're sad, you're sad; if you're pissed, you're pissed. But you won't stay there for long. It goes without saying that living with acceptance also means welcoming others and their journeys with an open heart. This includes people you love, and yeah, those you can do without.

> *Acceptance is appreciating who and where you are in this moment, warts and all, especially as you're growing.*

The trick is to figure out how they fit into your life and accept those roles. Will it feel immediately natural to travel out of your comfort zone this way? Nope, but acceptance will happen. It's like learning you have a gluten allergy and being told to replace the Barilla pasta with spaghetti squash for dinner. The change is out of character for you and even tastes sort of funny at first. But you also know the overwhelming benefits of a diet change, so you accept and make the best of it. Bake it like a lasagna, with fresh mozzarella, tomatoes, olive oil, garlic, and voilà—your appetite for positive change has you coming back for seconds!

You know who uses acceptance as a basis for just about everything? Kids. They're so incredible that way. Shortly after my Gramps died, I went to Maryland to celebrate my godson Ryan's fifth birthday. He and his cousin Sarah, who's seven years old, were sitting on the floor in front of the TV. Football was turned on for adults, but the kids were busy playing and not paying much attention.

At some point in the game, a group of servicemen and firemen opened an enormous American flag on the field, and this caught Ryan's eye. "Sarah, look what they're doing for Gramps!" he shouted, so excited. He went on to say that he was worried Gramps couldn't see the flag, because it was dusk and Gramps had bad vision when he was alive. But seconds later, Ryan spotted a bright light in the distance. "Gramps can see the flag now!" he exclaimed. "He can see it!"

What was Ryan thinking? Gramps was a fireman, and at his funeral, uniformed men from his firehouse acted as pallbearers and laid an American flag on his casket since Gramps had spent time in the navy. On their way to the cemetery, Ryan's family also drove under a giant American flag hung in Gramps's honor; it was suspended from two fire truck ladders, parked on either side of the road, and formed an arch.

So after making so many incredible associations between flags and Gramps, Ryan simply accepted that it always waved for my grandfather. The birthday boy had so much faith and acceptance in his heart—about Gramps's passing, how his soul could see us from Heaven, that the flag was for him, and how important Gramps was to have been given so many tributes by men in uniform (and on TV, no less!)—that I'll bet if Gramps in Heaven saw a light that night, it radiated brightest from Ryan. Acceptance illuminates the soul.

8

Don't Worry, Be Blessed

I'm blessed. You're a blessing! Bless, bless, bless, bless, bless. Enough already, people. Lately I've noticed that the term "blessing" and all its self-involved variations have become so overused and watered-down that a lot of you might not know what a blessing is anymore. Spirit and I would like to refresh your memory.

Blessings are exceptional and often surprising gifts from God that brighten your mood and add to your well-being. They're amazing moments that can affect you in insightful ways. A blessing always brightens your day, can change your point of view, and can validate or renew your faith in Spirit and the afterlife. And even when blessings seem minor in the grand scheme of things, they always resonate with your soul. Messages and lessons from Spirit during a reading are blessed by God, which also suggests that blessings give you what you need that day, even if you don't see it. Whether immediately or in looking back, blessings feel significant because they cause you to realize the guidance of a higher power.

Yet when we hear actors say during award ceremonies, "I was blessed to star in this movie" or trophy wives on the tennis court gloat, "God has blessed me with all that I have"—listen, I don't blame you for not knowing a blessing from bologna. Blessings are valuable and meant to be cherished and shared with others for encouragement. They shouldn't sound entitled, smug, vain, malicious, or as if God plays favorites by choosing to bless one person over another. You also can't choose whether or not you receive a blessing from Him or Spirit. What a crock! At least this isn't Spirit's take on the blessings I'm shown.

Blessings, All Around

Blessings come from God—let's start there. There is no purer origin. So when a pastor or priest blesses a congregation, you wish friends a blessed holiday, or you say a blessing before a meal, there's no question that these are holy efforts. They're given as an expression of His goodness and unconditional love. And while other Spirit might carry out a blessing as messengers—miracles can involve angels, a guide might help you meet a spouse, or a loved one's soul could give you a life-changing message during a reading—a blessing still begins with Him.

Loving children, answered prayers, a healthy family, and a stranger who waves you ahead at a four-way stop can all be blessings. The other day, a friend clipped forty-five dollars' worth of coupons when she was low on cash, and I feel that was a huge blessing. Now you might think, "God doesn't care if you get five dollars off toilet paper," but I don't agree. A blessing lifts your spirit and grows your soul.

Let's say God answers a prayer for support during the first Valentine's Day after your husband died. So your friends pool their money to buy you flowers and dinner, which makes you feel loved on a day that could have made you feel lonely or angry. You might go to bed laughing and grateful, remembering how they flirted with the waiter and ordered every dessert on the menu, just so you could have a bite of each. Those friends and their generosity are blessings.

God's blessings can also cause a domino effect that makes others feel connected to each other in a positive way. For my coupon friend, she used the money she saved on groceries to buy her daughter balloons to give her after her soccer game. This made her feel like a winner, even though her team lost. Their moods were so light that after dinner, they ate ice cream and snuggled on the sofa instead of doing their usual recap of what went wrong on the field. The coupons set off positive reactions that enriched an eternal bond and encouraged gratitude.

So how do you reap more blessings in your life? I don't know all the ways, but Spirit's shown me a few. Again, because God's intentions are untainted, Spirit's never said to me that you get more blessings based on how good you are. I don't feel like He's doling out blessings based on whether you're naughty or nice, like Santa! I do think God rewards faith and major steps in spiritual growth though, to encourage you to keep at it and spread the word about how much of an impact a blessing can have. I've also seen how the sheer act of expressing appreciation can raise your vibration and attract more positive things to you, including blessings.

Spirit says it's important to sincerely thank God for your blessings every day. You can do this during prayer, meditation, driving to work, walking to the deli—basically, whenever you get the chance. Being thankful also raises your awareness. Once you admit that you're blessed to have a warm home in the winter or a brother who makes you laugh, it'll become habit to recognize even more blessings in your life. That doesn't mean you have to literally count your blessings like that purple vampire puppet from *Sesame Street*—it would take forever, *ah-ah-ah-ah-ah*. But it helps to have an appreciative spirit, so you can recognize God's blessings as you encounter them.

God also gives you opportunities to receive blessings with your free will, which makes it your responsibility to make something of them. Blessings are gifts, which means you have to accept them and figure out how they fit into your purpose and lessons. When Spirit chooses to channel your mom or grandfather out of four thousand people at my live show, so that you can heal from grief to make tomorrow easier, that blessing is special. But it's up to you to really hear and benefit from the blessing. You also need to stay open to blessings, despite your expectations. Spirit might put a soul mate in your path, but if you're set on marrying a brunette and not a blonde, you might miss the blessing under your nose.

Spirit likes to send signs when a blessing is in your orbit, so be on the lookout for them. I know a woman who put a lot of effort into trying to work for a prestigious fashion website that she admired. She had an impressive interview, but they stalled on an offer. In the meantime, she got a call from a competitor whose job didn't interest her as much, but she took the meeting. Spirit sent her signs that this second job was for her, including the fact that she kept meeting random people who worked at the company and were very happy. So she trusted Spirit, took the job, and even scored a $25,000 signing bonus that helped pay for her wedding! But the woman wouldn't have received these blessings if she hadn't benched her should've-would've-could've's and accepted the gift with faith and optimism.

Before I forget: Spirit says you may not notice or accept a blessing if you need emotional or spiritual healing, since these factors make it difficult to recognize good things when they happen. Guilt, anger, grief, and other negative feelings can blind

> *Guilt, anger, grief, and other negative feelings can blind you to seeing or accepting God's gifts. So if you haven't felt blessed in a while, that might be a clue that you need to heal and grow a little first.*

you to seeing or accepting God's gifts. So if you haven't felt blessed in a while, that might be a clue that you need to heal and grow a little first.

Tough Times, Tough Blessings

It's easy to recognize positive blessings, but the blessings that come from hardship? They're more troublesome to spot, because you don't feel their benefits right away. A chronic health diagnosis, for example, naturally feels scary and upsetting; but it might also inspire you to blog about your condition, which urges you to find effective treatments more quickly so you have something to write about! In turn, this helps others by giving them advice, support, and community. Or hearing that your catty neighbor started a rumor about your marriage might push you to initiate a new friendship with a person who's more honest and understands you better. And while some material rewards can be blessings—like a work bonus that you put toward charity or a family vacation—not all possessions and achievements are. I know incredibly wealthy and accomplished folks who've earned everything they have with shifty values or by hurting others to get ahead. If these peoples' souls eventually learn lessons from their questionable choices, then there's the blessing, but the actual cash, clothes, and houses are not.

When Spirit validates its presence during a reading, they like to use blessings without always calling them that. And if you truly can't see past your grief to heal, Spirit makes it their mission to validate with blessings that open you up to feeling better. They itemize fun activities that you did with a loved one, inside jokes that made you smile, and special memories that strengthened your relationship. Spirit might even remind you of how you two used to blast music and dance real crazy or chase fireflies together—all blessings that speak to your soul. I read a mom named Su in Peoria, Illinois, who lost her son Zach in a car accident. Zach's cable was out, so his friend Andrew decided to drive them and Ashley, another friend, to Andrew's house to watch the TV show *One Tree Hill*. On their way, Andrew crashed the car into *a lone standing tree* on a country road, killing all three people instantly. OK, seriously. That coincidence is just creepy.

When I approached Su, she looked so terrified that she waved me and her blessing off in the beginning of the show, so her son's soul suggested I come back at the end. Spirit told me this woman had basically given up—she never laughed anymore and had begun losing friends. She was sobbing so hard that she couldn't make eye contact with me. When I eventually read her, Su's grief felt so raw that I could swear her son died yesterday, even though he'd passed seven years prior.

Zach's soul immediately said to me, "Please remind my mother of the stuff I loved to do in the physical world, because she forgot all those things." In other words, *Let's call out a few blessings now, so she's able to embrace even more gifts from God.* Spirit then showed me Su coloring, doing projects, and playing sports with her kids, and making cookies with them. I said to her, "Your son tells me you were always there for him and the rest of the family, that they always came first." His soul made me feel that this message was an enormous blessing for Su, since it validated that we were communicating and that he valued her role in his life. Su feared she let Zach down as a mom, and hadn't done enough or had done things wrong while he was alive, but his message put her at ease.

Zach wanted Su to find happiness and replace forced smiles with real ones. Now when Su is out, she runs into people who were at my show, and before she knows it, is remembering the good times with Zach all over again. I'll add more to her story when I talk about God, because Zach's soul referenced Him too, but for now you can see how Spirit sent Su blessings to feel better. They urged her to begin the healing process that Spirit wants for her and her soul needs.

Please, Sir, I Want Some More Blessings

I was taught that blessings can multiply and watching this happen in person is so freakin' incredible. Now, it's one thing when Spirit piggybacks, allowing many people to receive similar life- and soul-changing messages. But when they guide me to readings on a certain "theme," I watch blessings increase before my eyes! It reminds me of how ladybugs hibernate in your house during the winter, then one day you spot one on the windowsill, and a few hours later, they're in every room!

When I was in Charleston, I read a man named Louis who'd never seen my TV show, but had several friends who had kept on him to see me live since he'd lost both his parents. Louis's dad died thirteen years prior and about a year after his death, his soul came to Louis in a dream, said he was OK, and sailed off in a big Cadillac like the one he'd always driven; Louis felt this meant he's at peace. But it had been a while since Louis's mom died from pancreatic cancer, and he hadn't heard from her soul and feared it was because he'd been self-medicating; if she were trying to connect, he thought his fuzzy aura might've blocked her efforts. Then almost a year to the date of her passing, a girlfriend said his mom came to her in a dream with helpful and accurate medical advice for Louis's partner. This encounter moved Louis to buy a ticket to my show two months later, where he serendipitously ran into his friend! Talk about signs . . .

At the event, Louis's mom's soul gave him the most incredible validations right away. She referenced softball, and Louis confirmed that he'd been working hard on a celebrity softball game for his nonprofit's signature event. Her soul also knew he was about to marry his partner of fifteen years at City Hall in Washington, D.C.; this was also true, though he later changed the location at the last minute (a nice example of how Spirit gives us free will). Not one to be left out of a blessing, Louis's dad's soul chimed right in. "Your mom and dad are saying how proud they are of your work and of the man you've become," I told him. "They also love your

partner and are proud of you both—they will be at the ceremony."
When I caught up with Louis later, he said to me, "I cannot tell
you how much that reading meant to me. My parents were there to
say 'be happy, heal, keep the faith, and always reach out to us. We
are here.'" *Love* that.

But the blessings at this show didn't stop there! The next guy I
read had also lost his mom, and her soul said she was proud of him
for losing almost 650 pounds. Right after that, I read a teenager
named Peter, who was upset about his grandmother's death. "But
there was another loss, right? Something big, but not so sad," I
said. That's when Peter's mom said that he'd lost 78 pounds!

If that weren't enough, Spirit said a person in the audience
was connected to a weight-loss foundation. I couldn't believe my
ears. Louis raised his hand once more and said, "It's me again! The
nonprofit I mentioned is for obese kids, called Louie's Kids." Shut
up! Turns out, Louis's father was morbidly obese—never less than
400 pounds, 550 at his biggest—so Louis works to keep kids from
struggling down the same road his dad did. Clearly, the emotional
impact that his condition had on Louis ran deep. "Having a dad
so large meant never getting my arms all the way around him for
a hug," Louis said later. "He'd watch games and practices from the
car in the parking lot, which I think he did so he wouldn't embar-
rass us. When I graduated high school, he waited for the celebra-
tion at home. It wasn't easy for him to do stairs, and we never really
went into restaurants because I think he felt ashamed. He was an
incredible dad, but he struggled."

Chronic conditions have far-reaching impacts on family and
friends, so it's no wonder Spirit banded together to connect the
three men at my show under one theme, to encourage healing. Af-

terward, Peter told Louis how touched he was, and Louis encouraged Peter to share his journey with the kids at his organization. Let's just say the blessings for these three had more layers than a low-fat yogurt parfait, hold the granola! The messages helped their souls mend and mature, jump-started lessons, and then multiplied like freakin' biblical fish by introducing three guys to each other who share a major commonality. If you ask me, these are the people who should shout from the rooftops, "I feel so blessed!"

9

The Best Gifts Keep on Giving

Nobody likes a gift more than I do. Listen, my husband, Larry, has kept me in earrings and nameplate necklaces for most of our marriage—it took me twenty-eight years to break the man in, and now he's exactly the way I like him! But gifts that symbolize love and appreciation don't just come from the living. You can also get them in the form of sentimental keepsakes that were left for you or emotional messages sent "high priority" from the Other Side (blessings are also gifts, as I've mentioned). The other gifts Spirit refers to are the unique abilities you're meant to use in the physical world that add to your happiness and nourish your purpose in this lifetime. Their application should have a spiritual component to it that benefits your soul and other people in some way. And whether we're talking gifts you can actually touch, or how your talents touch others, the common denominator is that all gifts are a way that we can connect with one another—and therein lies the lesson.

When FedEx Delivers from Heaven

When I read clients, Spirit's primary goals are to teach lessons, lift burdens, and work on healing. But as someone who likes *stuff,* I think it's extra fab when Spirit talks about the tangible things they want you to cherish in their absence!

When a person dies, it's fairly common for you to redesign or repurpose the possessions this loved one left behind. Spirit thinks it's awesome that we honor them like this, and when they tell me that they like what you've done, their excitement channels similar to what it would feel like if they'd handed these items to you themselves! Whether you're turning Dad's flannel shirts into a quilt or your great-grandmother's diamond ring into three solitaire necklaces for her nieces, Spirit beams every time. During a live show in Connecticut, I felt drawn to a group of strangers seated together, and as it turned out, all owned creative reinterpretations of keepsakes that Spirit wanted to discuss. One woman had her husband's gold wedding band melted and reshaped into a heart, with the engraving still on it. Another turned her aunt's fur coat into a mink stole for her wedding (I was proud of myself for reading that, because I don't even know what a "stole" is. I've never been given a fur. Just sayin', Larry . . .). I was also impressed with a camouflage backpack that a military dependant made from her husband's uniform. It was cool too, the kind of thing Vic might like for school. I sensed that Spirit

> *Whether we're talking gifts you can actually touch, or how your talents touch others, the common denominator is that all gifts are a way that we can connect with one another.*

seated these women together so they could talk about their inventive gifts after the show, again, to encourage support, if just for that day.

I find that Spirit's gifts are always thoughtful and knowing—they put the "special" in "special delivery"! One of my favorites arrived when I read a young woman who was seven months pregnant. Her father died when she was a child, and his soul told me she always talked about "Grampy" to her baby bump and couldn't imagine being a mom without having him around. Then he spilled that the pregnancy wasn't planned, at which point I assumed ol' Grampy was a ridiculous gossip. So I said to the woman, "Um, was this baby a surprise?"

The woman started laughing and told me that not only was her pregnancy unexpected, she'd never planned to have children—like, ever! I realized, then, that her dad's soul had only the sweetest intentions. He asked me to tell her, "This child is exactly what you need." What I didn't say aloud was that Spirit wanted to give her a positive focus, a person to love and care for in his absence, and a reason to get up in the morning because it's such a rewarding commitment to care for a child. Because our souls choose our families to help them and us learn lessons, I'm sure her father helped his grandson's soul choose his mom. "Theresa, don't tell her this is my fault," he said, laughing, "but this baby is a gift from me!" Looks like Grampy's secret is out.

So what is Spirit teaching you by bringing up, or sending you, gifts? For one, they want you to know they're still involved in, and aware of, what's going on in your life. And when they talk about changes you've made to valuable items, that's also Spirit's way of letting you know they support all the choices and decisions you've made related to their passing. They might begin a message by referencing a lighthearted choice, like resetting a necklace, and then segue into a heavier one, like selling a house, donating clothes, or making medical decisions prior to their death. But the gift thing isn't just a lesson about the past. It's about always trusting your instincts to point you in the right direction, and realizing that Spirit knows what your soul needs, just as that father's soul did for his daughter.

Gifted and Talented

Every one of you is born with gifts that revolve around being able to appreciate life and what you contribute to it. I always say, you only remember living once, so you're cheating yourself if you don't make the most of your soul's time here!

Your personal gifts can involve an enormous calling like feeding the poor or finding a cure for cancer, or a more intimate purpose, like mentoring children, making people smile, or caring for a sick friend. But no gift is too trivial or seemingly mundane. One way to discover your gifts is to think about what you already do that makes you feel good (yes, you can do this while soul-searching, meditating, laying on the beach, Om-ing in yoga class, or during any quiet moment really). I don't mean what you've been told you're good at, or what friends and family appreciate your having done for them, but what makes you excited. I'll bet your whole life, people have been implying or outright telling you what your gifts are, but as your soul grows, you'll get closer to figuring them out for yourself.

This isn't to say that the jobs or roles you have right now are bogus; in fact, I'll bet there's something about each one that keeps you going, and that kernel is what I want you to think about more carefully, because it could reveal a hidden gift. You don't have to turn your gift into a career either, but you should devote time to it, so that you can get more in touch with what makes you, you. Maybe you paint murals in homes, but the best part of your job is greeting the pets you meet at each one. Why not paint dog portraits on the weekend? If you're an executive assistant who keeps candy in a bowl at her desk, and gives sharp advice when people swing by to grab a mini-Snickers, I can assure you that typing one hundred words a minute is not your gift. More likely, your gift is knowing what to say at the right time, and to whom. This doesn't mean you have to start a line of candy-scented greeting cards, but you can help yourself and others by volunteering at a hotline for troubled teenagers or training to be a certified life coach. And if you're just in it for the sugar rush, why not make some extra cash scooping ice cream after work or taking a pastry class? Sounds like a yummy life to me!

Gifts Are for the Soul

From a spiritual perspective, we're all here to learn service to others and we can use our gifts to do that. Making the most of these talents shouldn't feel like charity, though. At the very least, enjoying your gifts can be a small service, since when you're happy, everyone around you is too. Your talents are also at their best when they intertwine, though certain situations may only call for one or two. Beyond mediumship, I feel I'm good at being compassionate, generous, and kind. And when I work, they support my abilities. But obviously there are times when only compassion or kindness is necessary, and those moments are no less important. Like when I'm in the supermarket picking out tomatoes, and the woman next to me asks if I think the ones she found are too soft or look spotted and rotten. By exercising kindness and generosity, I might give her a few of the denser, more fragrant ones I chose, but I don't *have* to start channeling her dead family too (though, let's face it, I usually do).

Like the best guidance counselor, Spirit wants you to live up to your potential and believe in yourself. Of course, you can't believe in yourself if you don't know who you are, which takes us back to why it's important to never stop soul-searching. And because your gifts are linked to your purpose, Spirit doesn't want you to force or copy another person's abilities, even with the best intentions. This reminds me of how a lot of my clients use their gifts to honor loved ones. Maybe an organized mom starts a foundation related to the disease her daughter died from, or a numbers-savvy nephew expands his uncle's landscaping business after he dies. Spirit appreciates these efforts, but you can see where knowing yourself is helpful here; they don't want you to lose who you are in the process. Years ago, I read a sixteen-year-old boy whose father had died. He wanted to feel closer to his dad by walking in his footsteps, so he considered becoming a police officer. But during his reading, Dad's soul reminded him of a path that was more true to his son's passions and purpose. His soul said, "Thank you for wanting to carry on my legacy, but that's not you. You always wanted to be a gym teacher. Do *that*

> *We're all here to learn service to others and we can use our gifts to do that.*

in memory of me, so you can reshape people's lives in a way that only you can."

It's hard to accept sometimes, but Spirit tends to guide you to situations that challenge or force you to use your gifts, so you can learn lessons from them, make people's lives better, and reach your soul's fullest potential. So the next time a situation stings, remember that it's likely for your own good and a bigger plan is at work. During a live show in Hartford, Connecticut, I read a wife who used her caretaking abilities to nurse her dying husband, until he passed and gave her a gift that grew his soul and hers. (By the way, this woman was one of eight who'd lost their husbands, seated all in one section of the theater. To each wife, I found myself shouting, "You lost a husband!" and "You lost a husband!" and "You lost a husband!" I sounded like the love child of Oprah and the Grim Reaper!)

The first thing this woman's husband's soul said was that she "did things for me that a wife should not have to do for her spouse," meaning she cared for him more like a nurse than a partner. "And with all her health issues," he continued, "I always came first." The wife then explained that she has cancer and confided, "I didn't take care of myself when I was caring for my husband, because he didn't want me to leave him." I could feel the soul's gratitude and remorse. "I now realize that despite your struggles," he had me say, "you put them aside and did everything for me, and never once did I thank you. For that, I am sorry."

Spirit then bestowed on the woman and her family a final, moving gift—an explanation to a nagging question. His soul said they'd always wondered why the husband died first when the wife's diagnosis was far worse. Spirit explained that actually, his soul left the physical world sooner in his destined block of time so that his wife could get well and care for herself again. "My children need a mother," his soul said. "My death gave you life." The woman sheepishly admitted that her doctor said she was improving. I explained that her husband's soul made this choice in real time; his physical self didn't consciously choose to die. The wife had already learned her caretaking lessons, and fulfilled that part of her purpose, but neglected herself in the process. So her husband's soul opted out earlier in his destined window than it originally planned.

Spirit's gifts are priceless, and surprising, and can bring you to tears. But you will never regret what they teach you. Each is more meaningful than the last.

10

Intuition Ain't Just for
Psychics Anymore

Do you consider yourself intuitive? What? No? But you are! And your intuition is the most precise, immediate, and effective way to learn about your soul and connect with Spirit. I feel that everyone has a certain level of intuition, and I believe you're meant to use it to lead a guided and purposeful life in the physical world. I talk a lot about intuition in my book *There's More to Life Than This*, so I'm going to try not to repeat myself too much here. If you'd like practical advice on how to improve your intuition or safely open a connection to the Other Side to communicate with Spirit, that book is a great companion to this chapter. Otherwise, let's talk about what intuition is and how it relates to learning lessons.

I like to think of intuition as a personal navigation system, like a GPS for the soul, but one that actually works and doesn't guide you to Timbuktu with a robotic English accent. Intuition provides assistance and direction from Spirit, but the extent to which you use this tool to communicate more intimately with Spirit is up to you. Because you're here to learn lessons and enjoy God's gifts, I feel the most compelling reasons to develop your intuition are to use it to be of service to others, to be true to who you are, to grow your soul, and to make the most of each day and encounter you have. Not everyone is put on earth to talk to dead people with their intuition, but everyone can use it to guide them at work, in relationships, with their families, when making important decisions, and so on. Every role you have in the physical world relies on intuition that's made better by spiritual guidance.

Basic Instinct

Intuition manifests as the thoughts, feelings, coincidences, and emotions that pop into your head and nudge you to behave a certain way or avoid things that are bad or dangerous. Has an internal voice or sudden impulse ever told you to call one doctor over another, not get on an airplane, or take a specific job—and you later came to realize that that was, in fact, the best decision you could have made? That's intuition! It's a sixth sense, a sense of "knowing" that comes from within. Intuition isn't unpredictable and it doesn't occur randomly; it's deliberate and divine guidance. You also have free will, so you can choose not to listen to these signals and do your own thing instead. But if you want the most fulfilling life you can have, listening to your intuition is a good way to avoid feeling stuck or overwhelmed with negativity. Spirit's guidance only wants you to live well.

Intuition comes from Spirit, including guides, angels, loved ones, and God. In addition to a sense of knowing, I can often tell who's communicating with me by the images Spirit flashes in my mind; they're like the holograms on *Star Trek* or at a Tupac or Michael Jackson concert! I don't expect this happens when you get a hunch, unless you're psychic, but I'll touch on what I experience just in case.

I was taught that our guides, which can include angels, provide us with most intuition, instinct, coincidence, random or fleeting feelings, and intervention in times of danger. So I'll see angel wings when a feeling comes from my angel guide Solerna. If it's from my other main guide that I call Chief, I'll see an Indian headdress. If I get direction from a loved one, I might see an image from an old photo or just their head or torso. When I'm guided by God, I see white light and His energy feels calming, serious, and the highest of any I channel. He's way beyond holograms!

The other thing about intuition is that it's never wrong, though it may take you in a roundabout direction to where you're meant to end up. I have a client named Alison who, years ago, was at a crossroads about who she should marry. She felt she had a choice between two men, her boyfriend or a new guy she'd become very close to, and she admittedly felt her intuition pulling her toward the new flame. So she ended her old relationship to start over, but within weeks her evolving dynamic with this other guy made it obvious that she'd made a rash and poor decision. Their chemistry was only strong when their bond felt illicit, and they didn't have as much in common as she'd thought. Alison went back to her boyfriend, rekindled their love, and they've been happily married ever since.

When Alison told me this story, she was confused about Spirit's guidance in it. Did her intuition screw up and send her down the wrong path? No way. Spirit actually showed me that Alison is the type of person who needs firsthand experience to know when she makes the right decisions; she likes proof. Without it in her relationship, she would have always wondered about being with that other guy. So Alison's gut instinct didn't misguide her; Spirit just gave her the guided tour to where she was supposed to be all along. It's interesting too, because Spirit told me that this kind of indirect guidance is similar to what they give you when you follow your instincts to choosing different medical treatments that ultimately don't save a person's life. Similar to Alison's situation, Spirit knows when you need to feel you did everything you could do, even when nothing could be done.

Guidance isn't always obvious, but if it were, you'd never have to intuitively search for meaning and, thus, learn many lessons. In fact, misfortunes like suffering, tragedy, and sickness are especially linked to soul growth, because they force you to lean hard on what you feel instead of what you think you know. And if you could predict guidance's outcome with certainty, Spirit also knows you'd never feel the rush of a pleasant surprise, and what fun is that? For example, if you feel drawn to buy a Lottery ticket at the local 7-Eleven, this doesn't mean you'll hit the jackpot. You could bump into an old friend, grab a drink, and reconnect in a great way. Or, on the other hand, you might be like my friend Lauren, who was at 7-Eleven when my face came into her head. She took it as a lucky sign, bought a scratch-off, and I'll be damned—she won five hundred dollars! Forget a rabbit's foot; you should put my face on a keychain. And though these similar scenarios have different outcomes, intuition pulls through for both.

What's hard is when you think you're making a decision with

your gut, but it's really coming from your brain. This teaches a lot about self-reflection and, frankly, most people only realize it in retrospect unless Spirit knocks them over the head with a sign. I remember when my friend Kate took her first job out of college at a business magazine for sporting goods retailers, though she graduated top of her class and wanted a highfalutin position at *The Wall Street Journal* or *The New Yorker*, which was more her style. Kate kicked and screamed about the opportunity at first, but since the money was good and the people were nice, she told herself she'd stay a year then get out. Imagine her surprise when she stayed five years, climbed the ranks, and used her background to land a job at a prestigious business magazine!

Kate thought she initially ignored her instincts and her career path worked out anyway, proving her gut was way off. But she later realized that taking a more impressive job on paper would have been the rational choice. It was her survival *instinct* that made her take the job for the paycheck and peers, and as it goes with intuition and guidance, the decision happened for a reason and paid off.

Brains, Guts, and Spirit, Oh My!

Because intuitive guidance isn't always obvious, Spirit shows me that you should still temper your intuition with some rational thought. You aren't meant to bet the farm on a hunch. To use my client Alison as an example, if she'd stayed with the wrong guy because she hung on too tight to that initial feeling that they were made for each other, even though they weren't, she would have missed out on marrying her soul mate. A lot of people assume that intuition lets you understand or interpret a situation without using reason, but you need your brain to help make decisions too. I think a lot of weird things, and then my brain realizes it's just Theresa making shit up. Like when my son, Little Larry, was a baby, I constantly freaked out that he'd overheat, not eat enough, eat too much, and go flying out of his baby swing. But this wasn't intuition; this was neurosis. Logic would have come in handy.

Many of my best decisions have struck a balance between intuition and rational thinking, like the best family vacation we ever took. My instincts said to vacation in the Turks and Caicos for the sunshine and coral reefs, and we sensibly went for Victoria's Sweet Sixteen instead of throwing her a party. This way we were able to justify the cost by thinking of it as a two for one deal!

I also think it's telling that when I channel, I do my best when I lean on my intuition one hundred percent, but in everyday life, I have a less accurate "success rate" when I don't combine intuition with some reason. Like I didn't help Little Larry choose a college solely based on intuition; we researched the best programs, took campus tours, met professors, and then let our instincts help make the final call. Listen, I wouldn't even buy a blouse based on whether my instincts alone told me I'd look good in it; I'd try it on first, check the price, and make an educated choice. Don't get overly caught up in looking for signs either, or asking Spirit every little question, like if you should buy skim or two percent milk

Let your intuition guide you, but also use your head and take responsibility for the free will choices you make.

at the store. Let your intuition guide you, but also use your head and take responsibility for the free will choices you make.

Don't Just Listen to Your Intuition, Trust it.

Intuition is a sense of knowing, but you have to trust that what you know is real. The best way to learn how to count on your intuition is to try it, and then practice using it a lot. Choose a situation maybe at work, in love, or with your finances—where you tend not to make the best choices. Then find a day, week, whatever works, to use your intuition as a guide. You can ask your gut questions during meditation or as they arise in your day, or just follow your impulses. You can also think of a question, and then shuffle through possible outcomes and see which sparks the strongest sense of knowing. Don't expect to see a blinking YES! or NO! sign in your mind's eye, but I suspect that Spirit will send you subtle cues that you're on the right track, and then you can take everything you know and combine it with your intuition to determine how to make the next move.

Learning to follow your intuition is a lesson in letting go and relinquishing control. In no time, I'll bet you'll be walking through life with trusting and knowing, instead of questioning and fearing. Intuition is like the spiritual reflex of a healthy soul, just as your gag and knee-jerk reflex are the involuntarily movements of a healthy body. Instinct should automatically kick in when you need it to.

When it comes to using your intuition to connect with Spirit, young children have a special knack for this. That's because they don't doubt, make excuses, or second-guess their experiences. Little ones are also the best example of why you can't *only* let intuition run your life, because if kids were allowed to solely live by their gut feelings, they'd eat candy for breakfast and smack their siblings for no reason! Children's inspiring ability to accept Spirit's messages reminds me of two boys I met, both of whom miss their grandfathers very much.

The first is named Logan, and he was almost two years old when his grandfather died. I learned about him while reading his grandmother Pam and Auntie Bee in San Jose, and Spirit showed me that Logan always talks about his "Papa," especially when he plays alone in his room. As I channeled Papa, his soul explained that Logan does see and interact with his spirit. Papa also showed me that his family had recently stayed at his favorite resort in Waikiki. At school, Logan was taught to say "Pumpkin pie!" during picture taking, and throughout that Hawaii trip after Papa's death, Logan added his own twist every time the camera went off—he'd say, "Pumpkin pie, Papa!" Logan instinctively knew his grandfather's soul was on that vacation with them, and Spirit told me the same.

Another time in Nashville, I read an eight-year-old named Landon who also calls his grandfather "Papa." (OK, honestly, what are the chances that my two favorite kids for this section have grandfathers nicknamed "Papa"?) Landon signed up for T-ball shortly before his Papa died when he was three years old, and one of the last things Papa said before he passed was that he wished he could see Landon on the field. Sure enough, Landon told his family that he's seen Papa's soul at his T-ball and now baseball games, either on the field or in the stands, and sometimes in the clouds. When I channeled Landon's Papa, his soul validated that he had been to all his games and said Landon is an excellent catcher! He even told me about his favorite green bat. Landon does, in fact, love his bat with its green graphics, which he named the Green Monster. "I think about Papa all the time at baseball now," he said. "I know he helps me from Heaven!" Never once has Logan or Landon doubted their Papas' presences or the sense of knowing they feel that their souls are with them—and hey, look how Spirit rewards them!

Even if you don't use your intuition every day, Spirit's told me that it's especially sharp when you're struggling. You just have to tune in. Once at a live show in Connecticut, Spirit told me there was a woman in the audience with old photos from the seventies in her pocketbook, and as it turned out, she was sitting right in front of me. The pictures were sepia-toned and looked worn around the edges from being clutched all the time.

Spirit said the woman's mother died when her daughter was young and that she asks a lot of questions about what Mom was like; nobody will share much, since her mother committed suicide and the topic is taboo in her family. So Mom's soul showed me that when her daughter is shopping and finds herself wondering if Mom would like this or that, she asked me to suggest that she listen to her intuition. During these feelings and questions, the soul said it will be with her and speak through her thoughts, emotions, and instinctual responses. It will be like her mother is whispering, "Yes, that's what I'd like. That's what I *am* like."

Spirit uses your intuition to communicate with your soul, because it is the core of who you are, will be, and everything you value. Isn't it time to listen?

11

Learn to Read Sign Language

A lot like the jeans in my closet, Spirit's signs come in all shapes and sizes. A sign can be anything unusual, strange, or coincidental that makes you think of a loved one, since it's their soul that usually sends it your way or directs your attention to it. You can also get signs from other Spirit—including angels, guides, and God—when you ask for direction in a crisis or for reassurance that you're on the right path. Just as you stop or yield when you see road signs, Spirit asks you to break when you encounter their signs too. Granted, you won't get a yellow triangle with Uncle David's head on it, but Spirit's signs always grab your attention. I think of signs as friendly and comforting hellos from Heaven, validation of unbreakable bonds with souls in the afterlife, and proof that Spirit is with you at the exact moment you receive a sign. Even better? The more you notice signs, trust them, and spiritually mature, the more you'll be aware of these amazing gifts.

You know that Alanis Morissette tune called "Ironic"? My

cowriter heard it on the radio when we began this chapter, and it made us want to rename the song "Symbolic." The lyrics are about searching for meaning in the unknown, especially when you encounter curious signs—a black fly in your Chardonnay, a traffic jam when you're already late, a no-smoking sign on your cigarette break. Alanis sings that *life has a funny, funny way of helping you out,* which is what Spirit does when they reassure us with symbols. And yes, I'm sure it was a synchronistic sign that Kristina heard this when she did! So the next time you hear this nineties tune, change the last line of each verse to say, *And isn't it symbolic . . . Don't you think?* You'll get a more spiritual message, loud and clear!

The bottom line is that signs—ironic and otherwise—carry a lot of meaning. They're linked to lessons, so you should learn how to interpret, embrace, and hopefully grow from them. Next time there's a bug in your wine, consider what Spirit's trying to tell you. Nanny, my dad's mom, sends me big, fat flies to show that her soul is around, so you and Alanis wouldn't be the first!

Signs I Can Get Behind

People always ask me how they can be sure that a sign is honest and truly a sign. When is a frog more than a slimy amphibian, or a flickering light not just a sign that you need to change the freakin' bulb? Those are fair questions, and it feels wrong for me to tell you to blindly trust that you'll know a sign when you see one. Yes, faith is part of understanding and receiving messages from Spirit, but that's easy for me to say, because my faith is validated every day. I can "see behind the curtain," so to speak, and I don't want you to feel that I take this for granted.

I thought about my experiences with signs and realized there are four key factors that describe most signs: the *S*ign itself, the sense of *K*nowing you get when you see it, the *T*iming of it, and the *R*eassurance you feel as a result. You can even think of these as the acronym SKTR—you know, like my son in high school, when he grew out his hair, carried a longboard, and used words like "ollie."

So first, let's discuss the sign itself. Some of the more typical ones I hear about include animals, insects, feathers, songs, smells, loose change, and religious articles. But a sign can be anything that connects you to, or reminds you of, a loved one. If these signs come from other Spirit, your intuition and the context will hint at whom they are from. I personally get a lot of signs and guidance from my grandmothers. As I've said, Nanny sends flies, and Gram, my maternal grandmother, sends dimes and bunnies. In fact, the day Gram died, a bunny hopped off her front stoop, darted in front of my car, and looked me square in the eyes before crossing the street to disappear. Ever since, I've seen bunnies when I need encouragement, speak to Gram in my head, or when she's just on my mind. But you have to understand, a sign doesn't mean the soul is that thing. Gram isn't the bunny, though Larry would love that, since he's crazy about animals and always wanted to be a veterinarian. He'd keep five furry Grams as pets if I'd let him! No, Spirit just uses things like bunnies to get your attention and let you know they're with you. Their souls don't reincarnate *in* the signs or anything.

Another important point is that signs aren't just objects. Synchronicity can be a sign. Spirit can also mess with your electricity, turn your faucet on and off, fool around with toys, or make objects tilt, move, or go missing. You might notice repetitive or lucky numbers on a clock, as a house number, on license plates, or as phone numbers. Numerical patterns can be personal, like a birthday or anniversary of a death, or have universal meanings like 111, for example, which is a sign that divine intervention is happening or about to. Spirit can make loud sounds, like clanging, knocking, or footsteps too. And if Spirit is physically close to your body, you could feel chills, pressure, or an air-tunnel effect in your ears, or a tingly sensation on your head. Spirit might even touch you, or direct your attention to someone who looks like a loved one. All unusual, all meaningful, all signs.

A lot of people identify with the same sign, but no two signs are exactly alike, because a sign's meaning is so personal. Take butterflies, for instance—a lot of you see them. Yet years ago, I read a woman who lost her husband and son, and had a very unique experience with this insect. During the woman's reading, Spirit showed me that she often saw two butterflies together that seemed to chase her wherever she went. The woman freaked out when I told her they were a sign from her son and husband. And then more recently, I read a lady who couldn't stop thinking about how her mother died. Her mom's soul asked me to tell her, "I wasn't alone, and I wasn't afraid. Your father greeted me when you left the window open." I had no idea what the window reference meant, so the daughter explained that her dad died twenty-two years ago and was buried in the cemetery across the street from her parents' house. As Mom's body shut down, they opened the window to feel a breeze and a butterfly flew in and sat above her; when Mom took her last breath, it fluttered right back out and across the street to the cemetery! Shut the front door (and while you're at it, the window)!

In both these stories, Spirit used beautiful butterflies to symbolize souls on the Other Side, and the fact that they're with loved ones there. But in the first example, the creatures wanted to demonstrate that the souls are safe, at peace, and still with family in a different way; in the second, Dad wanted his daughter to know he greeted Mom's soul when she passed. Both helped reinforce their faith.

> *A lot of people identify with the same sign, but no two signs are exactly alike, because a sign's meaning is so personal.*

Knowing and Timing Are Everything

For me and my clients, I've noticed that signs come with a sense of knowing and incredible timing. This knowing happens when you see a sign and feel a confident response that it's connected to a loved one or guidance. It's a sharp *a-ha* and feels a little like recall. So a cloud isn't just a cloud if it's shaped like an apple, you called your wife "the apple of my eye," and your gut screamed, *OMG, that cloud looks like an apple! OMG, my wife! OMG, that's crazy!* Or if you heard your son's favorite song as you drove past the cemetery where he's buried, and your belly did somersaults. You'll know who's sending the sign because there'll be a natural association between the person and the sign, like with the apple or song, or if there's no obvious link, a name, feeling, or image will come to you.

As you feel a sense of knowing, you'll simultaneously recognize that it's important when the sign occurred too. Maybe you were just thinking of Uncle Fred or asking God a question in your mind, when the sign appeared shortly after or a few days later. My client Karen told me how she came home from work one evening, desperately missing her husband John who'd died three years prior. She flipped on NBC's *Community*, took a shower, and when she got out, no joke, the TV was on ESPN—John's favorite channel. And how about when my cowriter had tech issues with our tape recorder during this chapter? After asking her guide for help, she looked outside the window and saw a robin staring right at her; it sat peacefully on its branch until the problem was fixed, and then it flew away. She intuitively knew it was Heavenly aid, and of course, the timing tipped her off too. You might also get signs when you don't expect them, but Spirit usually has a reason for dropping by, even if it's just to say hello or isn't immediately obvious.

Spirit usually has a reason for dropping by, even if it's just to say hello or isn't immediately obvious.

The final benchmark of a sign is reassurance. That's the main intention behind most signs—to show you Spirit's present, encourage hope, offer assistance, and reinforce valuable lessons about patience, acceptance, and trust to name a few. You can't always sit with a medium or communicate with Spirit all day, so this is their subtle way of encouraging you and reinforcing beliefs. Spirit's guidance and comfort might not even be entirely for you, but still affect you in a nice way. One Valentine's Day, a client told me her husband sent flowers with the card, "I'm so glad you're mine," when she also happened to buy him a cupcake that said, "Be mine." It was a strange coincidence because these two never spoke about their marriage with words that indicate belonging, but that afternoon, when her friend called to say she was fighting with her controlling boyfriend, the cupcake and card were suddenly a godsend. They prompted my client to talk about the difference between being "mine" in a safe and loving way, verses "mine" in a possessive and threatening one. The sign cued her into knowing how to help her friend, while reinforcing that her own relationship is in a healthy place.

So what should you do when you get a sign? Say hi, tell the soul you miss or appreciate it, share news from your life, express gratitude, or simply say "I love you." You don't need to have a long conversation. Acknowledging Spirit's presence is plenty. And for the love of a higher power, please don't overthink the meaning of each symbol. Though Spirit's messages can feel like a riddle, the signs they send leave a very obvious impression. Feathers or footsteps, bunnies or butterflies, Spirit wants you to feel their presence, cooperation, and love.

One Sign Leads to Another

I've noticed that if you don't have strict expectations about how Spirit "should" send a sign, it's easier for them to do so. Don't accept any random occurrence as a message, but don't close yourself off from less obvious signs because of unrealistic expectations either. Spirit doesn't always send signs that match your memories or hopes, but they're usually in the ballpark (for instance, there's no need to ignore a yellow finch just because Mom loved red ones). A lot of people also ask if they should set up some kind of system with loved ones while they're alive—*Send me a groundhog! Play me the song "Sweet Home Alabama" on a Tuesday!*—and that's a fine idea. But Spirit connects with us based on how we see and feel Spirit, plus how Spirit is able to communicate based on a few factors, including the soul's vibration. So if a soul doesn't have the energy to do what you've planned, or you don't interpret signs that way, you could miss a message if they send one that was unplanned. The good news? Spirit almost always shows up and their signs can be better than you imagined. I had a client who found twenty-dollar bills every week or so from her husband's soul. Forget pennies from Heaven. This big spender sent Jacksons! You think the wife signed up for life insurance from the Other Side? Of course not, but she embraced his gifts as a sign that he's still looking out for her in the afterlife.

You can ask or pray for a sign if you need comfort or guidance, and while you should be specific about prayer requests, don't be demanding about the sign itself. *Send me three signs by five p.m. Show me red roses, because white won't do. Use images in my mind's eye only.* That's so unfair. Plus, you think Spirit doesn't have other things to do than send you flower holograms and feathers by sunset? Request a sign, release it with faith, and move on. Spirit doesn't always get right back to you, but you'll learn patience in the meantime, and that pays off too.

Just like you, I appreciate clear and obvious signs—as does my family. When everyone's together on holidays, they always want to know if Gram's with us, and we have a lot of fun talking about the signs she's sent lately. So the week before Thanksgiving one year, I said to Gram's soul, "What I'd love for you to do from now until Thanksgiving is make your presence known to everyone who'll be at dinner, so they can have their own experiences to share." I felt that Gram's soul was more than happy to play along and boost everyone's spirits, so on Thanksgiving, we went around my mom's table and talked about the signs we all got from Gram. My brother pulled a dime out of his pocket. My cousin Keri had a different place setting than the rest of us but it was an identical match to the set she inherited when Gram passed (in fact, my mom had only one duplicate because she got it as a gift from a friend).

When it was my turn, I told everyone how I'd visited Gramps at his rehab center on Thanksgiving, just before dinner, and when I went out to the courtyard, I heard a Romanian musician playing the xylophone. He sang in another language, but after a bit, he transitioned to "You Are My Sunshine" in English, which Gram used to sing to us kids! I sensed that her soul was at the concert with us, and as I was leaving, an older lady playing marbles said to me, "Spirit wants me to tell you to have a happy Thanksgiving." I didn't even know this woman! So yes, I receive signs from Spirit much like you do. I guess Gram's soul could have literally sat next to me at the concert to make me feel her energy, but she sent me my Thanksgiving signs the same way she did everyone else's.

When Souls Grow, Signs Change

Signs aren't just fun to notice and talk about; they're directly linked to spiritual growth. When Spirit uses lessons they've learned to help us heal, like during a reading, our improvement and their messages raise their vibration. This helps them communicate more accurately and in new ways. Also, as we improve here, our souls grow and intuition strengthens. So when it comes to signs, the most mature souls give and receive the most advanced signs. See, I told you it pays to heal!

Clients who see me after years of processing a person's death often say, "I feel so much better, but I'm not seeing signs from my loved ones. They used to send owls and pennies, but not anymore. Is everything OK?" I find that you get as many signs as your soul needs, but Spirit also sends new and more advanced signs when their energy gets stronger. Sometimes you have to notice the change. For example, my friend Anna used to smell her mother's Chanel No. 5 all the time, but lately, she's discovered her mom's possessions in the strangest places. In one week, she found Mom's old prayer card in the pocket of a new sweatshirt and a gold bracelet, which she hadn't seen since her mother died, got caught in her dresser drawer and almost chipped the groove! Her mom's soul had to work hard for the energy needed to move objects like this; she wanted her daughter to notice!

So what signs show the greatest growth? Spirit says one of the more advanced signs they can send involves making their energy feel solid, like when you feel a soul touch you or sit beside you on the bed. You might feel hands on your body, lips on your cheek, or see an indentation on a bed's surface as if a person were making it. I've noticed, too, that clients who lose kids or spouses tend to experience solid energy a lot, though I'm not entirely sure why these souls seem to be stronger than other loved ones who depart. I feel like it's related to the love they share and the intensity of their bond, but I can't be certain.

Spirit sends new and more advanced signs when their energy gets stronger. Sometimes you have to notice the change.

My friend Regina Murphy, whose son Brian died in a drowning accident and was the first child I ever channeled, recently lost her husband, Bill, as well (Bill contributed a lot to my first book, in case you remember him from there). And Regina gets regular visits from both souls, separately and together. She says Brian gives her a hug and kiss on her right cheek every day—"it feels very gentle, like he was"—and Bill hugs her with "the strength of a man, not a boy," and it's usually on her left side. Regina can also feel when the two embrace her at the same time, because she feels pressure in two spots that are near each other. And on the night Bill died, she felt his and Brian's hands on her left leg, which was full of pins and needles from their energy. I've always known that Brian and Bill were strong souls, but Regina's role can't be underrated here—she's receptive to their signs and trying her best to heal, as well. Their connection as a family was powerful in this world and continues into the afterlife. Spirit relies on this union to bridge the two.

12

Be Your Own Dream Catcher

In Native American tradition, dream catchers are made from a willow hoop and decorated with arrowheads, feathers, beads, and other artifacts from everyday life. Hung above or near the bed, it's believed that these objects have the power to literally "catch" and filter your dreams at night. The web is thought to protect you from negative dreams while letting positive thoughts enter your mind.

I feel very connected to Native American beliefs, and I mention dream catchers because they remind me of how your mind is susceptible to good and bad thoughts when you sleep. When your brain is at rest, it's easiest for Spirit to communicate with you, and if you're sleeping, this often means through dreams.

Spirit has shown me that they can send you positive messages and guide you to your lessons, and aspects of your purpose, through dreams. By connecting with you this way, you can reach the truest part of yourself and souls on the Other Side, especially if you're plugged into your intuition. I love that all dreams allow you to explore your past, present, and give you future food for thought. They're creative expressions of your highest self that teach, heal, and make you smile, knowing that Spirit is forever guiding and protecting you, even as you slumber.

To Sleep, Perchance to Learn

A lot of mediums and spiritual teachers have firm beliefs about what happens when we dream. Some feel your soul leaves your body and travels, others think dreams use universal symbols that show how we all share a consciousness, and most say you have the ability to shape your future through your dreams. I only bank on what Spirit tells me, which is that dreams can offer guidance and reassurance, and can help you to learn lessons; they often direct your attention to areas of your life that need it. When I began working on this chapter, Spirit showed me that dreams can also be a kind of meeting place for you and Spirit, when they want you to feel comfort, know they're OK, or want to connect "face-to-face."

If that's not insane enough, Spirit says you can visit the past in a dream or predict the future, not to stop an event from happening but to prepare you for when it does. I'm sure there are other reasons for souls to star in your sleeping life, but those are the most useful and instructive. Listen, everything in the human body has a function, and the part of your mind that creates and processes dreams is no different. On a spiritual level, I feel our brains and souls work together to help dreams do their many tasks, including connecting this life to the next one.

I have to say, spiritual folks also love to split hairs about all the different types of dreams and visitations out there, but I don't care what they think is real or not real, or if a dream fits into a neat little box. I'd rather focus on the interactions people have with Spirit when they seem to be sleeping, and the purposes these serve. This contact is technically considered a visitation, but it can happen in the context of dreams and feel like real life is occurring within a dream . . . so, I'm going to simplify this in my own way. From now on, I will refer to the soul's appearance as a visitation and the context as a dream. Capiche? Capiche, because Spirit also tells me dreams don't have to be strictly one thing or another—a visitation or a dream, a past-life experience or a premonition, soul traveling or a fantasy. A dream, however, can most certainly contain aspects of each, since Spirit's priority is that you look at visitations and dreams from a positive perspective and use your intuition to see how they fit into your life to make it better.

I believe all dreams are meant to put you at ease and give warnings or clues into what you're thinking and feeling subconsciously, but I don't think you have to talk to Spirit to have a spiritual experience. Plenty of enriching dreams are long and rambling. They can be a jumble of thoughts, images, ideas, and feelings that make sense after you analyze them. They may reflect emotions, wishes, or be a mash-up of what happened that day or relate to a movie you watched before bed. But if you can pull out even a small lesson or fresh way of seeing an issue from these dreams—well hey, that's valuable insight.

Dreams are also a great source of ideas. Listen, where do you

> *Dreams don't have to be strictly one thing or another— a visitation or a dream, a past life experience or a premonition, soul traveling or a fantasy.*

think inspiration comes from? Intuition, namely your guides. In fact, lots of famous works of art were based on dreams, like the Beatles' hit "Yesterday," Salvador Dalí's melting clock painting *Persistence of Memory,* and many of Edgar Allan Poe's poems and stories (on second thought, maybe Poe could have used a dream catcher!). So don't think non-Spirit dreams are useless to your soul, because they're not. At the very least, you might wake up with a ridiculous story that makes everyone laugh at the breakfast table, which raises their vibrations.

I know this is a chapter about dreams, but I don't want you to get too obsessed with dreaming, because some people dream all the time, others don't dream at all, and this isn't the only way to hear from Spirit or peek into your soul. Besides, if Spirit really wants to get a message to you through a dream, they'll find a way. When my client Margaux lost her mother-in-law, Luisa, her soul communicated with Margaux's babysitter, Dianne, because Dianne's sensitive. (In fact, the morning Luisa died, Dianne suddenly dropped a teacup and the words "Rest in peace" flew out of her mouth; this happened at 6:21 a.m.—the exact time Luisa died over four thousand miles away.) Luisa came to Dianne in a dream, holding a beautiful navy blue suit and said, "Make sure Margaux doesn't throw away the blue dress. Tell her to keep it to remember me." Dianne asked if she had anything else to say, and Luisa simply said, "Good-bye." Well, the only piece of clothing Margaux has of Luisa's is a navy suit she gave her years ago—and Luisa always referred to her suits as dresses. Even better, the night Luisa came to Dianne, Margaux's husband was upset that he couldn't find an item that was, and I quote, "suitable" to remember his mom by. Hearing the message put him at ease.

As for Margaux, the dream led to a spiritual awakening—not because of the message itself, but because of what it represents. "I have a deeper understanding of how God and the universe work, and Luisa's visitation forced me to reconsider how I employ and understand my faith when a loved one is dying," she said. "Believing in God and His entities isn't about using them to save people, but leaning on them for support. I need to feel grateful for the time I have with loved ones here, while I have it. And when I attend church, I'm reminded that there's more to life than we can see, touch, and rationalize with our logical minds." This is a great example of how a dream can be a catalyst to growth, just because it gets you thinking; the lesson doesn't need to directly relate to the dream's message or plot to have an impact.

Mr. Sandman, Bring Me a Loved One

As with Luisa's obvious intentions, Spirit rarely delivers puzzling messages during a visitation. They're usually short and to the point. A visitation can include a quick exchange, a few sentences, or a word. Spirit might stand there without talking, or the message's meaning may be understood without words since souls communicate through thought. Across the board, however, you'll always remember Spirit's messages, clear as day.

That being said, there are times a loved one appears in a dream that feels confusing. The most common way a visitation throws you is when you can't tell whether you're awake or asleep, dreaming of fiction or reality. You might dream that you're doing exactly what you're doing in real life—lying in bed, maybe facing a certain way, and either awake or sleeping—except in your dream, you're also interacting with Spirit. This happened to my client Jill, the night after her grandpa died. She lived in Key West at the time and couldn't afford to fly to London for his funeral, since she'd seen him in the hospital a few weeks earlier. She felt really upset and conflicted about this.

Then Jill had a dream where she felt like she was asleep and had woken to see her grandpa standing over her. "It looked like him before he was sick," she told me. "He said it was OK not to fly home and that it was great to see me before he died, which was more important than being at the funeral. Then he faded." Jill assumes that she woke up after that, though she wasn't aware of the transition from sleep to wake, because she was awake in the dream and her body was laying the same way. What felt most curious was that after the experience, Jill's bedroom in real life smelled like her grandfather—you know, the unique skin smell that people have and you recognize in those you care about.

One thing I love about Jill's story is that it shows how most visitations require little, if any, interpretation, but if you're grieving or carrying guilt, your fears could easily cloud it. If Jill's grandpa hadn't told her it was fine to miss his funeral—if he'd just stood over her, looking dapper, saying nothing, and then disappeared—she might have thought he was upset with her, particularly if she'd felt negative emotions related to his passing or about attending his funeral. But with all visitations, this is never the case. Are your loved ones smiling

> *Most visitations require little, if any, interpretation, but if you're grieving or carrying guilt, your fears could easily cloud it.*

in the dream? Happy? Healthy, like before they got sick or died? Then they're saying that's how they want to be remembered and want you to know that it's all good in Heaven.

If a dream seems meaningful but still bewilders you, ask your guides for help interpreting it during meditation or a quiet moment alone. But don't make yourself nuts with this process, please. Treat dreams like you do a hunch when you're awake: don't blow it off, but don't overthink it either.

Healing Visitations: Band-Aids for the Soul

Nine times out of ten, visitations are meant to be lessons in healing, so it's invaluable when they let you spend time with a loved one after they've died. My friend Regina, who I've mentioned lost her son Brian, dreamed about Brian shortly after he passed, when all she wanted to do was hold him one more time.

In the dream, Regina stood in front of a sea of people with blurred faces in a bright green meadow with vibrantly colored flowers that, to me, sounds an awful lot like Heaven. Then two people with blurred faces stepped forward from the crowd and handed her Brian as a toddler. He cuddled into the nape of her neck like he always did, and she was filled with so much love. Regina breathed a sigh of relief and woke up. She told me she knew this was a very real experience and a gift from God. I also sense that Spirit was assuring Regina that she'd interact with Brian's soul in the future and experience his unconditional love, which she still does. At the very least, it was a lesson in support, intuition, and faith.

If Spirit senses that you'll hesitate to move on without them, they may visit you in a dream to tell you that they feel it's time to begin healing. I mentioned my client Karen earlier, and a few weeks after her husband, John, died, she slept on his side of the bed and had a dream that symbolized what a hard journey Spirit knew it would be for her to accept his death. Karen dreamed she and John were at her grandparents' house, which, in the dream, she felt represented Heaven.

Crying, Karen told John's soul that she needed him to come back with her. "Karen, you know that isn't possible," John said. "You know I can't be with you. You have to go on your own." She left the house as he stayed inside and watched from the door. Karen began walking alone, down a street that became a scary neighborhood, and a creepy old man drove behind her in a car. She was terrified. Karen ran back to the house where John was, stood on the front steps, and pleaded to him through a screen door. "John," she said, "this world isn't safe for me. I cannot do this alone." But John comforted her with a clear, visitation-like message: "I promise I'll never let anything happen to you."

When Karen woke up right after, she knew she'd be fine. She also said it felt like she'd traveled to a real place to talk to John, although it happened in the atmosphere of a dream and didn't feel like she'd made it up in her head. Me? I think her instincts are spot on.

Dream a Little Dream of Spirit

Spirit wants you to feel protected and reassured, so they're not above name-dropping if it'll console you. Praying or speaking to certain souls of faith may also make them more likely to visit you in a dream than a loved one, or even a guide who you might not recognize, since the point of a visitation is to help you feel instantly content. When this happened to me, it was an awesome experience.

Spirit gives my brain the night off, so I rarely dream of anything—not even a funky recap of my day. I basically go to sleep and wake up six hours later. But I did have a visitation while sleeping on the acupuncture table! I heard that this actually happens a lot because acupuncture removes energy blockages, so it might eliminate the blockage that exists between us and the Spirit world too. Anyway, I was under a lot of stress with work and really on edge. I'd already lost my voice, couldn't breathe, couldn't sleep, and I was crying a lot. So I went for acupuncture, and even with all those calming needles in me, I felt an anxiety attack coming on. I bolted up and said to Antoinette, my practitioner, "You have to help me! I'm freaking out! Please don't leave the room. Just stay with me." So Antoinette asked if she could sit beside me during my session and rub my hands until I fell asleep (I always nap during acupuncture). I liked that idea a lot.

The minute I was in dreamland, I saw a bunch of Catholic saints surrounding my acupuncture table—Padre Pio, the Infant of Prague, Saint Jude, Saint Anthony, and Saint Teresa—with Mother Teresa standing at the foot of it! It's like, *Gang's all here!* I didn't communicate with these Spirit, but I did feel an overwhelming sense of peace and confidence that I'd be OK. At the end of my session, I had to tell Antoinette what had happened. You know what she said? "I prayed for you the entire time you were asleep," she told me, "and specifically to those saints for healing and relaxation." Come on, that's crazy. Even for me!

Dreaming in Past and Future Tense

Some dreams are generated by your superconscious mind, which is also used during past-life regressions, and may be why it's possible to visit a previous life in a dream. I have a client named Kristy who has a recurring dream that she's on a playground; kids are hugging her legs and calling her a name she doesn't recognize, though she knows it refers to her. The kids are also on a roundabout—one of those flat discs you spin by pushing on its handles, running in circles, then jumping onto it. When I told this to my friend Pat, who does past-life regressions, she said the children were likely referring to Kristy as they knew her in another life; they may have been repeating the name to remind her of that experience. Pat said the next time this happens, Kristy could ask them why they're calling for her and what lifetime they're from. If you ever have a similar dream, you should do the same! I'm no expert on past lives, but I'll bet Spirit gives you access to these dreams so you can learn from them in some way, don't you think?

Now, when you see the future in dreams, or have a "precognitive dream" as it's called, Spirit is often doing this to prepare you for an upcoming trauma or to validate how strong your intuition is. My friend Regina has precognitive dreams, as did her husband, Bill, when he was alive. "I'll all of a sudden be living in a sequence of events that is exactly the same in every detail to my dream," she told me. "As they occur, I'll compare the events around me to still shots of the dream in my head." Bill described precognitive dreams as HDTV, with intense colors and clarity, compared to watching a snowy black-and-white set from the fifties. "It's like you're living the event, rather than dreaming it," he said, "and perhaps in a way you are." While awake, Bill also received a cue when the dream was about to become reality, like a sound, smell, word, phrase, or color. He also felt extremely alert.

Bill had many precognitive dreams, from predicting a meaningful visit from his uncle as a kid to foreseeing details about his son Brian's life after Regina became pregnant. When she was four months along, Bill had a precognitive dream with details that crack me up. He saw Regina's OB wearing a black surgical cap with Bugs Bunny in the center, Daffy Duck to the left, and Elmer Fudd on the right. This seemed strange, since the same surgeon wore blue scrubs when he delivered their other two kids. Fast forward to Brian's actual birth, and this doc wore blue scrubs *and* the cartoon cap Bill saw. As Bugs might say, "What's up, Spirit?"

When One Dream Says It All

Every once in a while, you'll have a wonderful dream that hits the Spirit jackpot—they tell you how they look and feel great, pass on a meaningful message, and show you that their soul is at peace but still around you. Bill did this with his son Dan in a two-part dream. (I know I'm using a lot of Bill, Brian, and Regina stories, but with so many incredible encounters, I can't help it!) First, the night before Bill died and he was in a medically induced coma, his soul showed itself to Dan wearing his hospital gown, with gray hair and a gray beard, looking very sick. He then slowly transformed to being young and healthy. His hair and beard gradually changed to jet black, and he was in regular clothes. Bill didn't speak in the dream, but Dan knew his father was telling him he's OK, and Bill slowly walked away.

A few weeks later, Dan had a second dream where Bill appeared with the same jet black hair and everyday clothes. This time, Bill seemed frustrated. He was standing in front of Dan and Regina, with Regina wearing a blindfold and headphones, as it rained down quarters. Just before Bill died, Regina told him she'd like to receive quarters from his soul so she'd know they were from him, and at the time of Dan's second dream, she was telling everyone she hadn't seen one quarter yet! The dream, however, told her Bill sent her signs, but she wasn't seeing them. She'd been distracted and incredibly sad. So get this—as Dan finished telling her the story of his dream, a quarter rolled down the side of his pant leg. I couldn't make this stuff up! Dan was standing and his hands were on the kitchen counter, so they were nowhere near the side of his leg. The quarter appeared out of nowhere! Bill literally made his family's dreams come true.

13

Angels Walk Among Us

I love a good angel story, don't you? Just hearing about how they're tasked to protect, guide, deliver lessons, and intervene with compassion and grace makes me feel so grateful and secure. They're a warm reminder of how the universe looks out for you, as they act on God's behalf and lead you to situations and choices that help you along your spiritual path. They are luminous teachers.

Angels are subtle yet powerful, influencing lives in critical ways and on a regular basis—not just when an extreme or nerve-racking situation calls for it. Contrary to what you might think, you don't have to wrap your Toyota around a tree or get trapped in a burning building to encounter an angel! Spirit says they're all around us, radiating positive, playful, and benevolent energy every day.

Angels 101

Angels are God's celestial messengers, protectors, rescuers, interceders—and there are vast numbers of them. Like all Spirit, angels are also made of energy and don't have solid bodies like we do. In Heaven, angels are fluid beings that move and change, and they travel through space like a feather that drifts through the air. Yet when they interact directly with humans or when intervention is needed, angels can take on the appearance of animals (as Native Americans believe) or ordinary people. Growing up, I also remember Bible stories about families who invited in a stranger, only to learn that the person was an angel. How's that for a reason to answer the door? Maybe your Avon lady has holier pursuits than selling lipstick!

Now, I don't know a lot of specifics about angels, since angelic details aren't that relevant to how I choose to use my gift, which is to help people heal, learn, and grow from Spirit. I also can't describe angels' physical attributes because I've asked to see Spirit without many features at all. I freak out too easily! There are mediums who purposely channel angels and/or ask to see lots of characteristics, but I'm not one of them. The only time Spirit shows me the face or wings of an archangel, for instance, is when it's used as a symbol or a client calls on that angel and Spirit asks me to validate it during a session. So if your guardian angel came forward in a reading, I'd see it as bright, angelic energy and feel that it has a higher and lighter vibration than a human soul. But that's it. Done and done.

I was taught there are various types of angels that include archangels, guardian angels, cherubims, seraphims, basic angels, and others. Spirit also tells me angels are responsible for over-seeing the many dimensions, universes, and galaxies in which we learn our lessons. They have a range of more intimate jobs and missions too, like encouraging and strengthening you, plus answering your prayers related to known angelic duties like protection and healing. And even if you don't practice a religion or believe angels exist, Spirit says they still watch over you. Angels are assigned to everyone, and some are with you throughout your many lifetimes.

My friend Bill Murphy had a unique relationship with angels while he was alive, and I can only imagine what it's like now that he's crossed over. Bill told me he met his guardian angel when he was four years old, at the bottom of a hill where he'd seen a pre-cognitive dream unfold and heard a soft-spoken adult voice say in his head, "Watch, learn, say nothing." Then, a few months later when he was riding his tricycle with his cousin in this same spot, he zoomed down the steep hill toward a busy road at the bottom. This is when Bill saw a figure standing in the middle of the avenue, and he remembers thinking the guy was going to get hit by a car if he didn't move out of the way! Bill actually wrote about this experience and his wife shared it with me. Here's what happened:

There was a man dressed in a long, dazzling white robe with a golden cord tied around the waist. He was taller than anyone I'd ever known, with long, blond, shoulder-length hair and the most beautiful face I'd ever seen. He just stood there, calmly, in the middle of the traffic, with his arms outstretched as I approached him in the intersection. When I reached the road, it was as if the traffic just stopped, and I felt as if an unseen hand took control of the handlebars and guided me through the ve-

hicles. I struck the curb, landed in the front yard of a house, and was knocked unconscious with broken ribs, a concussion, and shredded skin. Had I run into any type of vehicle, I surely would have died.

Bill didn't need me to tell him that the soft-spoken voice he heard after his dream, and the man he saw in white, were angelic beings—maybe the same one.

Most people think of angels as the winged, backlit figures in paintings, books, and movies, but Spirit says that when most of us are touched by an angel, it rarely appears this way unless you're meant to recognize it for a reason. Like with Bill, I sense that meeting and seeing his guardian angel the way he did was related to his future calling to make stained-glass angels for families who lost a child (the soul of Bill's deceased son directed him to these people in precognitive dreams). Otherwise, Spirit says angels prefer to fly under the radar. In fact, I received this angelic message when we were writing this chapter: "Our presence is subtle. It is not our purpose to announce ourselves. It's up to you to recognize the small miracles of the angels." I knew those weren't my words because they're in third person, and right after I said them, my Theresa brain kicked in and said that being an angel is like being in the mafia! If you're in the mob, you don't walk around telling people you're in the mob. Nope, you get the most done by staying out of the way. Same with angels. Bada bing, bada boom.

Step Aside, Ma'am. Let an Angel Handle This

I've heard a lot of stories from clients who survive the unthinkable and only come to later realize they have angels to thank. During readings, Spirit's told me that miraculous interventions are often orchestrated by angels and guides that send loved ones to intercede, if they don't do it themselves. A departed loved one might also become the "face" of an angelic rescue, since seeing your grandma's or cousin's soul would be instantly reassuring and let you know that divine intervention kept you safe.

Not long ago, I met a wonderful fourteen-year-old girl named Hannah nearly two weeks before she passed away from an aggressive brain tumor. It was Hannah's Make-a-Wish for her mom, Sue, to sit with me after she died so that Sue could connect with her soul, but I

A departed loved one might become the "face" of an angelic rescue, since seeing your grandma's or cousin's soul would be instantly reassuring and let you know that divine intervention kept you safe.

thought that was such an unbelievable gesture that I wanted to meet Hannah in person too. So Larry and I drove to her home in New Jersey and spent a few hours with Hannah's family, just talking, laughing, and telling funny stories. Hannah even introduced me to my first Dairy Queen Blizzard! Can you believe I've gone my whole life without eating Oreos mixed into soft serve? Anyway, that's when a fantastic angel story came up.

When Hannah was six years old, she and her mom were in a terrible accident. They were on the highway when a speeding car hit theirs on the driver's side. The impact sent Sue's car reeling, and they flipped over, landing with the driver's side sitting on a guardrail. Somehow, when the car landed, Hannah was in Sue's lap (Sue never understood how Hannah got there, since she'd never unbuckled herself from a car seat before). And because Sue's door was smashed, the two were trapped in the car.

After a few minutes, Sue saw five men in white uniforms emerge from a white van and run to her vehicle. They wore what looked like green lanyards around their necks, and Sue assumed they were gas company workers. The men told her everything would be fine and that they'd be right back. But as soon as they left, two new men who'd witnessed the accident helped them instead. They removed Hannah through her window, then pulled Sue out the same way. When the firemen, police, and EMS got to the scene, everyone was stunned that Sue and Hannah had survived the accident without any injuries.

Sue asked what happened to the men in the white van, but nobody knew. She looked into a wooded area next to the highway, and in the distance, she saw her grandparents who'd died years prior. They smiled at Sue and her grandfather tipped his hat. Then they were gone. "I've always believed my grandparents protected us that day, since our car was totaled and we only walked away with a few scratches," she told me. But Sue never understood about the men in the white van, wearing white uniforms, with green lanyards, until she told me the story.

Spirit told me the men were truly angels and the "lanyards" were actually green scapulars. If you're not Catholic, this is a single piece of green felt and braid with a picture of Mary on one side and Her Immaculate Heart on the other, with the words, "Immac-

ulate Heart of Mary, pray for us now and at the hour of our death."
There are a lot of stories about how people who wear this and
say the prayer experience healings and miracles. I felt that these
angels saved Sue and Hannah's lives, and also unbuckled Hannah
from her sturdy car seat to allow the rescuers to get to her easily. I
think Sue's grandparents appeared to reassure her that she and her
daughter would survive the accident.

Angels, Angels Everywhere

OK, so here's where Spirit's angel talk surprised me when I was
working on this chapter. I was initially taught that no angel has
ever lived in the physical world like you or most guides have, but
recently, Spirit showed me something different.

Now don't write me letters or nasty Amazon reviews saying
I'm a fraud because I contradict myself, because that's not what's
happening here. As my gift evolves, Spirit reveals new information
to me when they feel I'm ready to receive or share it. Sometimes
these revelations expand on what I know, or totally flip my prior
beliefs on their heads. And since I don't really channel angels unless it's necessary to healing, but I wanted to talk about them here
since you're always curious about them, I guess Spirit feels that
now is as good a time as any!

Bottom line, angels are freakin' everywhere. I've often wondered if guardian angels and guides are the same thing, and I've
always known that an angel can act as a guide, since I personally
have an angel as one of my two primary guides. But I now sense
from Spirit that there are many angels alive on earth, quietly walking among us as humans with angelic souls, which means that sure,

There are many angels alive on earth, quietly walking among us as humans with angelic souls.

a guide can also be a type of angel. I was also told that this is one of the reasons angels can seem so easily "disguised" as everyday people—a huge transformation doesn't always have to occur. The other thing Spirit showed me was that angelic souls are alive in every person on earth and that after a long period of time and many, many lessons, you can evolve into a type of angel. All of this is to say that angels live among us but also within us. Yup, you heard me right. We all have a little bit of angel in our soul, and that means you too.

Spirit explained it like this: Every living thing is a direct extension of God, including angels, which are among the most highly evolved manifestations of His energy. And as you know, you are also energy before and after you have a body. Now, when you cross over, your energy merges with God's and you're literally part of Him, just like all souls and angels are in Heaven (Spirit's shown this to me as one big, fluffy cloud that separates into many smaller ones). And while on earth, a piece of your soul remains part of God's but with the added challenge of a body that introduces you to new experiences that help you learn lessons. But from a soul's perspective, the only difference between an angel and human is that an angel's energy is closer to God's and, therefore, has more God in its soul than you do, since people here are not as spiritually advanced as angels are in Heaven.

To simplify this, picture two pie charts, one for a basic soul and one for a highly ascended angel. The initial soul begins with a sliver of God-like, or angelic, energy, then gradually fills in as you reach new levels of growth. Highly evolved angels, on the other hand, are almost entirely filled-in with God-like energy. Your soul is part angel, because that's where it begins and what it is going to be.

When you come to the physical world with a little angel in your soul, you're meant to harness it for good deeds—give, lend a hand, and do kind, selfless acts without payment or recognition. You're supposed to do all of this using the

> *Your soul is part angel, because that's where it begins and what it is going to be.*

abilities God gave you, though how you choose to use them is up to you. And what did I say angels are? God's Heavenly beings that protect, guide, intercede, spread good, and deliver messages. So when you do this kind of thing on earth, albeit on a smaller scale, you're accessing the part of your soul that's angelic.

While it's obvious how someone like a doctor taps his inner angel by healing patients, most of us access it more modestly. Have you ever stepped off a plane with suitcases, packages, cranky kids—and one of those electric carts stops to pick you up without a reservation? What a lifesaver, right? The driver himself could be an angel in human form, but it's more likely that the angelic part of a normal guy's soul might have just kicked in. And at the end of the day, does it matter? Goodness arrived when you needed it. So when a stranger fixes your flat tire or a neighbor offers you sage advice—and your instinctual response is "You're such an angel!"— know that it's not just an expression. It's the truth!

A New Level of Growth

So all that said, I'm inclined to think there are angels God created before humans that are purely angelic souls that never walked the earth, as well as angels that we should aspire to become. And when human souls graduate to angelic realms, who knows what their jobs are? Spirit says there are more than we realize. Apparently the term "angel" as Spirit shows it to me, is a much broader concept related to energy and soul growth than what art history or religious texts have depicted.

Spirit gave me a great metaphor to make this whole human-to-angel concept a little easier to understand. They showed me that the transition from a human soul with a little angel in it, to a soul with a lot of angel, is similar to how a regular soldier gradually becomes decorated from marked accomplishments. This is so smart because decorations are often related to acts of heroism, merit, or outstanding service and achievement—that is, the types of acts angels are said to value, just in everyday life. So if it feels impossible to imagine yourself as a glorious angel someday, aspire instead to become an increasingly decorated soul.

I'm not gonna lie—this blew my mind too. I still don't have all the pieces yet. When angels show themselves to humans, do they look like a person they once were? Can you choose what kind of angel you want to be, based on your natural gifts in the physical world? Am I an angel in a Long Islander's body and is my halo made of diamonds? I seriously have no idea about any of this. But now do you see why I don't bother to interpret Spirit as a black-and-white issue? The universe is much more complex than I am ever told at one time!

The Ultimate Benefits Package

You know that Train song "Calling All Angels"? In it, lead singer Patrick Monahan asks for a reason as to why things are the way they are and sings, *I need a hand to help build up some hope inside of me.* Well let me tell you—it's a shrewd move to suggest calling on angels for knowledge, guidance, and hope, because that's exactly what angels are good at. And when you need a lesson in understanding or faith, calling on angels will always deliver.

As I've mentioned, I have a guardian angel named Solerna who acts as one of my guides. She directs me on my spiritual path, brings me peace when I crave it, and encourages me to be playful. When I communicate with her, my mind's eye fills with a bright, white light and blue aura. She reassures me that everything I do and say is guided and protected by God. I call on Solerna for everyday guidance, but I think of her more as a pipeline to God than my other guide, Chief, so she's the one I ask for intervention or if I have an urgent request.

Your angels want you to address them and employ their abilities. If you have a request, all you have to say is, "I call on my highest angels and guides," then name it. And when you're in the same positive state of mind as the angelic realm, their assistance comes naturally, since they're characteristically happy, grateful, and accepting. So the next time you need a cab in a rainstorm or good news from your accountant, keep the faith and order up some spiritual 911. Your angels are waiting to hear from you!

14

You Got 99 Problems,
but God Ain't One

Most of my clients have heavy hearts, so it can be hard for them to fully embrace their loved ones' messages and lessons. But when I channel God, everybody listens—myself included. I never know what He'll say, but I know it'll be good!

I talk to God more than you may realize. I had my most memorable conversation with Him when I accepted my gift, and though we don't shoot the breeze daily, I do involve God in every important decision I make and check in regularly, just to be sure I'm doing this medium thing in the best way. And though I know God listens to me, I don't always hear back from Him. Sometimes I'll get a sign or feel an instinctual response from one of my guides, who can act as His messenger. But I know what you're thinking, and don't worry—it's really obvious when God speaks to you through me! What I appreciate most is that His lessons and requests are so simple and modest for a God who could ask for anything. If I had to describe His approach, I'd say it's plain and powerful. Maybe this doesn't surprise you, coming from the creator of the perfect blue sky and a serene first snow. But God is a commanding minimalist in nature, so why not life too?

Now, if you're curious about what God and Heaven are specifically like, according to what Spirit and God tell me, you should read my book *There's More to Life Than This*, because I really get into those topics there. But in this chapter, I want to lay down a few God basics and interpret the role I've seen Him play, and been told He plays, in your lessons. To be clear, I'm not speaking for God. I might be God's gift to Larry, but I have more perspective when it comes to the universe! No, I'd like to share what I feel matters, based on what God says and prioritizes during readings—foremost among them, love.

For the Love of God

We are all connected to God's brilliant light, guidance, and overwhelming peace. He is supportive, nonjudgmental, and protective. He is the creator of all things and infinite, unconditional love. It's this love that links you to your family and friends in Heaven, because we all come from His energy. No matter what you call Him, I'm told there's only one God. And from what I can tell, it doesn't matter what religion you are, as long as you choose a faith rooted in Him.

After you die, you're immediately at peace because you're with and part of God; and since He is unconditional love, every thought, feeling, and experience you have in Heaven revolves around this idea. It takes a very long time for your soul to grow toward God, and that development is closely guided by the souls and angels on the Other Side. And when it comes to being held accountable for your deeds on earth, Spirit tells me that God isn't the fire-and-brimstone figure that a lot of us assume Him to be. He is compassionate and caring, and I don't feel there's eternal damnation for the average, flawed person.

Because people affiliate God with religion, I only used to reference Him if a client asked, since a lot of you struggle with anger toward God and the pressure of organized beliefs. I completely get it. But while God and religion are usually linked, they aren't the same thing. God is a positive, pure, and good entity, and religion is a set of principles and practices created to serve and worship God. You can use religion to follow God's ways, but God isn't religion personified. He also doesn't play favorites with one faith over another. When you get to the Other Side, God doesn't say, "All the Jews over here, all the Catholics over here, all the Hindus over here!" Also, just so you know, I refer to God with masculine pronouns because it's the most common way, but God isn't a person. He is like all Spirit in that they don't have a sex, but if they show themselves to me, they may use human traits like gender or faces, so that you can recognize them.

When I experience God, I don't hear or see Him like we see and hear in the physical world, but I have connected with Him on a level that feels really different than when I channel other Spirit like guides, angels, saints, and

> *God doesn't play favorites with one faith over another. When you get to the Other Side, He doesn't say, "All the Jews over here, all the Catholics over here, all the Hindus over here!"*

your loved ones. His energy comes from the highest dimension out there with a big, God-like majesty. It's so wild. The most I've seen with my eyes is a bright white light with golden edges that fills the room and makes me feel surrounded by love and peace. (If you've ever heard me refer to "God's white light," this is what I mean and visualize when I meditate, channel, and ask for protection.) Then my knowing kicks in, and I'm certain it's Him. When I channel God, I become very serious, and I'm more careful, precise, and to the point. I usually crack jokes when I channel and act like my easygoing self. Not on God's watch, I don't!

You can talk to God through prayer, or less formally, in your thoughts. If you've never prayed before, I don't want you to feel intimidated by it; prayer should feel like the most natural thing in the world, because God is in all of us. I think of prayer as asking God for what you desire in a grateful way that assumes, with faith, that your request is already being answered. (So you pray, "Thank you for healing my broken ankle" verses "Please heal my ankle.") This is different than meditating, which is listening to Him and Spirit. Spirit also refers to praying as "praising a higher power." Spirit says it's perfectly OK to direct requests to souls of faith, angels, guides, and loved ones as well, because a lot of souls have divine abilities and direct contact with God. Different faith-driven rituals seem to be fine too, as long as they're done with a pure heart and positive intent.

I like to nurture my faith in church, but if you feel closer to God in your garden or on the beach, that's where you should spend time with Him. Personally, I like to hear the sermons, sing hymns, and come out feeling charitable and kind. I also feel at home in church, even if my religion doesn't fully support what I do. Naysayers forget that I speak to God, and that He literally told me the reason I was chosen to do this is because people need to hear about Him in a different way. You know, I can't help but wonder if there'd be more tolerance or respect for

> *I like to nurture my faith in church, but if you feel closer to God in your garden or on the beach, that's where you should spend time with Him.*

my relationship with Him if we lived in biblical times. But I don't focus on the negative. I listen to the gospel, apply it to my life, and protect my faith.

Your Lessons: What's God Got to Do with It?

So how involved is God in your lessons? As you know, God helped you create a basic outline for your journey, based on the lessons you were meant to learn in this lifetime. He also gave you free will as to how much, and how well, you follow through. People and situations are placed in your path, but it's up to you whether you choose to grow from them or not. God cares if you learn lessons, because He wants you to use your time wisely here. It's for your benefit, not His!

You can learn lessons the easy or hard way, and I think we tend to forget about the positive routes. For instance, I think that what's considered a "hard task" can be up for interpretation or based on your mood. A cranky man's rotten luck is an optimist's blessing in disguise. You're also quicker to notice a lesson that comes from a bad situation rather than a positive one. If sunshine makes you feel grateful, you might la-dee-da your way through the day, but never stop to wonder if it's meant to help you appreciate simple pleasures. You might overlook the lesson, because it felt so darn nice.

Did you ever have a tough math teacher or demanding coach? I'll bet their pop quizzes were rough and standards high, but think how much better they made you! Your journey is similar, but your taskmaster isn't exclusively God. Every hurdle you jump is done to move closer to Him, but that's because your soul chose a challenging track. The next time you face an obstacle, you might also consider whether it's so doom and gloom. Spirit says we make situations harder than they need to be, and the path of least resistance might be the most spiritual.

Remember too that when it comes to death, this is an agreed-upon choice between your soul, your guides, and God; it's not entirely God's call, as so many of my clients assume. The end of your life usually occurs when that soul, not the human, chooses to leave within a window of time called destiny. I'm told that this is also the case with children who get sick or die young. Their souls agreed to take on an illness for their growth or that of the loved ones connected to them. A lot of times when I sit with a client, they'll say, "I asked God not to take my mom/brother/child yet, and He did!" But God isn't kicking back in Heaven like, *I'll take . . . that one! Now this one!* He's not calling back souls the way you pluck chocolates out of a box—this truffle first, then that caramel. In fact, God isn't doing anything *to* us, but *for* us, and even then your soul is involved.

> *When it comes to death, this is an agreed-upon choice between your soul, your guides, and God; it's not entirely God's call, as so many of my clients assume.*

Trusting God is a major part of everyone's lesson, mine included. And hey, I know it's hard; it's not like you can hear His voice or read His body language to infer what He means! Yet as you rely more on God, life gets easier. I don't think it's a coincidence that when I accepted my mediumship, the first thing He asked me to do was trust that He'd love, guide, and protect me always. I also had to trust what came with His gift—that souls who walk in His light are honest and good and that what I do is His work. You have to admit, that's a lot to count on!

But as I soon learned, God never leaves you hanging. You always get the support you need, based on where you are at that moment of your life and what your soul's plan is, long term—even if it seems like a roundabout route or an awfully slow way to reach a goal. So like for me, when it was time to meet the guidance that came with my abilities, God did it in a way that made it easiest for me to accept. He basically went from most religious to least, since I struggled with how channeling Spirit fit into my beliefs. First, I heard from God, who said mediumship was a gift and part of my journey. When I questioned if He was really God, I saw Jesus. God explained that Jesus, as my teacher, would always lead me, and Jesus reassured me that I could trust God and not be afraid. After that, I met Solerna, my guardian angel, then finally Chief, my Indian guide. If I had different values or practiced another faith, I think I'd have met different guidance in another way—albeit one that would still help me to trust Spirit the most. Now my relationship with God is awesome. I even bought a sign in Malibu that says OUR FAMILY MUST BE GOD'S FAVORITE SITCOM. How perfect is that? I wonder if He binge-watches *Long Island Medium* with all his favorite angels on a Sunday afternoon. I'll bet Solerna brings the popcorn!

Straight from God's Mouth

When healing messages come directly from a higher power, I try to figure out what God's really trying to say, not just to that person, but to all of us in the physical world, so you can benefit too. On the whole, His biggest priorities seem to include love, compassion, and community, since a lot of His messages revolve around those themes. He doesn't speak in monologues or parables with me— just a few powerful, direct words that matter because they're from the creator of the universe and resonate with listeners. Also from what I gather, learning gratitude, service, forgiveness, acceptance, support, love, and faith are on His "greatest hits" list of lessons. I've noticed, as well, that He doesn't shy away from the fact that He's the source of all reality. God wants you to use the tools, gifts, and choices He gave you to navigate your whole learning experience— good and bad.

During a reading, God often thanks people when they do His work and sometimes tells them when they'll be blessed for their faith; for devout souls who have already crossed over, His energy might surround them to show support for how their time here was spent and is acknowledged in the afterlife. At a live show in Delaware, I channeled an outstanding young soul named Zach who was six years old when he was diagnosed with leukemia but lived ten miraculous years after that. In fact, his soul bragged to me that he should be in medical books because he lived longer than most experts expected. (After the show, his mom, Tamara, shared that Zach "died" twice for eighteen minutes, and his doctor was in the process of submitting his story to medical journals.)

Zach's soul was proud of his commitment to serving others.

In fact, the tower of Alfred I. duPont Hospital for Children in Delaware was dedicated to him, since he worked with the facility's CEO and its architect to design patient rooms while spending over two years there as a patient. Spirit then explained that Zach was involved in various charitable causes, which included raising over $18,000 for St. Christopher's, his primary hospital—$11,000 of which went to putting PlayStations in all the treatment rooms! He also worked at the local soup kitchen, participated in food drives, and raised money for cancer-related causes plus families to help them pay for transplants and hospital fees.

When I'm in a large venue, I don't like to talk about religion or politics. Faith is personal, and I'm not out to convert anyone to anything. But if God shows up, hello, I have to say it! It's not my job to edit what Spirit says, and when I channeled Zach's soul, I couldn't avoid God's energy. I felt that Zach's soul was surrounded by Him, before and after he left this world, and Spirit said he had a related purpose in both. Zach's soul then showed me that babies were drawn to him, and that his role here was to make them feel safe and loved, and in Heaven, he helps infants and children cross over. I saw Zach surrounded by the souls of smiling little ones, like that image of Jesus with children at his feet. Zach told me he's now pain-free and in good company. "All he talked about his last week of life was how happy he was going to be with God in Heaven," Tamara said.

Another thing God tells my clients is that it's OK to be angry or turn from Him, if that's what you need for a time, but to know He's not going anywhere. No matter how close or far you move from God, His love never changes, and He will always guide you when you're ready. He also doesn't want fury to obscure the fact that your loved ones' souls are at peace. God says all this because He wants you to heal and move forward. He wants the well-being of your loved one's soul to be your focus, because negativity holds you back from growth and serenity.

God tends to step forward when a person I'm reading isn't processing Spirit's messages, and I can almost hear Spirit clearing their throats, like, *Ahem! You'd better listen up, 'cause God is about to speak!* In Chicago, I read a couple whose two kids died in a camping accident. Grief was killing their bond, and although Spirit's validations were strong—down to knowing the father had giant freakin' tattoos of their faces!—I could tell that I wasn't reaching them emotionally. That's when God took over, and the family listened. "There is so much anger," He said, "but you have to support each other in this, no matter what happens to your marriage." By the end, I could tell from the way they exchanged knowing glances that they'd turned a corner. It was a small one, but God'll take it.

If you want pure and powerful, the most impactful lesson I've channeled from God is this: "I exist. I'm real. I'm here." That gives me the chills! I've felt and "seen" Him, but it's a whole other ball game when I can feel and see a change in you because of God's presence. When I was in Peoria and read that woman named Su I talked about in chapter eight, her son, Zach, celebrated God's existence in front of the whole audience. (Crazy—two Zachs in one chapter. God must have a thing for this name!) Like Tamara's Zach, Su's son had a very strong spirit. His soul had a lot to tell his mom, but he really needed her to know about God. Su had been questioning her life's value and struggling with whether Zach was confused or lost in the spiritual world somewhere. The young man's soul spoke simply but clearly when he said, "Mom, there is a

God. And there is a Heaven." Su was beside herself. "Zach confirmed my belief about God and Heaven," she said. "I also needed to know that he was safe in God's arms

> *The most impactful lesson I've channeled from God is this: "I exist. I'm real. I'm here."*

and felt peaceful to know he was." You can't ask for a warmer embrace, or welcome home, than His.

15

Spread the Love

I love me some love. From an arm around my shoulder to a dog's wet kisses, nothing beats the way a caring gesture makes me feel all warm and fuzzy inside. And because God's energy radiates love, and is found within our souls, Spirit says we all have the capacity to give a tremendous amount of love to ourselves and others. Yet so many people feel like they have to search hard for love or give it out sparingly. It shouldn't be that way. Relationships are like mirrors—reflecting your strengths, shortcomings, and showing you who you are at that moment. So if this is the case, do the people in your life make you "look" good and loved?

Spirit talks a lot about how your relationships are related to your lessons and journey, especially since our souls are interconnected and relationships are interdependent. Life has given us so many opportunities and reasons to appreciate one another and make each other better. And no matter how busy I am, I try to always appreciate the people who affect me throughout my day.

Whether I'm buying strawberries at the farmer's market or going over my schedule with my assistant, every exchange connects me to someone who depends on me as much as I rely on them. So how much better would every interaction in life be if at least some aspect of it were influenced or impacted by love? Really freakin' better!

Love, Love, Love, Love . . . Crazy Love

Love, in its most honest and pure form, is the most extraordinary and inspiring feeling you can have and express, but it can also be misunderstood, manipulated, and miscommunicated because it is so powerful. You can make choices in the physical world, or others can make choices affecting you, that get in the way of love's integrity. A painful childhood, for instance, can make it hard to give love and cause you to seek out love too much or from the wrong people. But role models for how to love each other the right way shouldn't escape us. Inspiration is literally everywhere. Open a religious text, watch an elderly couple share a pastrami sandwich, or turn on the radio (love songs inspired this chapter's subheads too). Love is also beautifully unique. You don't love your mom the same as your brother or partner. And even when love hurts, you come back for more because the soul is hopeful, and most of us have known how good it can be.

We tend to think of ourselves as independent human beings, but I don't think anyone is solely responsible for who they are and how they

> *Even when love hurts, you come back for more because the soul is hopeful, and most of us have known how good it can be.*

love. So many people and events change and encourage you, and it's interesting to think about how they've influenced what love means to you. Even if your dad is a pain in the tuchus, or a sibling takes advantage of your loyalty, they've informed who you are and are becoming. The next time you're alone, maybe driving to the store or raking leaves, think about this: If you won an award for your ability to understand love, who would you thank in your acceptance speech? And while you're at it, what would you wear? (That last part's not a spiritual question. I'm just curious!)

Spirit wants you to put love into everything you do, from talking to an irritating salesman to doing volunteer work. I'm lucky that so much of my job is motivated by love, in that I adore what I do, who I work with, and genuinely appreciate the clients I do it for. Find ways to pursue what you love and contribute your love to the world too. Use love as your motivation and inspiration to do more than love your spouse or raise your kids; love outside the box. My mom, for example, always cooks with love. Whether she's making chicken soup or sausage bread, she carefully chooses the ingredients, thoughtfully layers them in, and serves the result with such pride, you'd think she'd made a third child.

Spreading the love doesn't have to take much time. One of my favorite Internet posts is a bunch of photos that shows people lovingly devoted to simple, kind gestures. There's one of a man reading to his blind coworker on a lunch break, another of a guy posing with a bag of bagels he gives to hungry people on the street, and then my favorite, a shot of free quarters taped to index cards that say "Just give," "Enjoy the moment," and "I hope I made you smile." The best part is that they're stuck on gum, toy, and candy machines! Do you know how excited my kids would have been to find this at our local five and dime? What an excellent lesson on how to make the world a cheerful, silly, and welcoming place!

Make You Feel My Love

Accepting and giving love is a choice, and there are endless opportunities to love and be loved every day. I'll bet your personal trainer, the waitress at your favorite diner, and your car mechanic are all open to trading love. I'm not saying you have to make out with Sal, the guy who rotates your tires. But appreciate these folks, do something nice for them. It will make you feel less alone and, yes, full of love.

Love is a wonderful way to pay it forward. I've heard that the more love you give, the more love you get back—but it works in reverse too. The more love you get, the more you give to others. When you're comfortable with how love feels, you're not afraid of reaching out to new people and because you're happier, you act more loving without even trying! It's also easier to love yourself when you know how it feels to be loved. You become a person others want in their lives, and you want them in yours. You spread the love, without even trying. At the end of the day, I think we should all follow the love, as much as we can, the way Toucan Sam follows his nose to a bowl of Froot Loops. Just like that bird's famous striped beak, your heart "always knows" when it's on to something good!

When a loved one passes on, Spirit likes to teach that demonstrating love can be as simple as listening and saying how you feel. Unfortunately, a lot of souls I channel don't learn how to express love until they reach the Other Side, review their lives, and learn lessons there. But don't wait, if you can help it. Once I read a woman who'd lost her husband, and his soul asked me to tell her, "I wish I'd told you how much I loved and appreciated you. I learned from Heaven that I never said that enough." Then he laid a dozen red roses in front of her and said, "I want to show my love and devotion." Funny enough, his wife said he sent roses on their first Valentine's Day together when they were teenagers, but never again. He had a hard time saying "I love you." She goes, "Instead of this, he'd say, 'You know how I feel by what I do.'" During her reading, his soul finally said *and* showed his love. Hand to God, Valentine's Day was less than a week away.

People think the opposite of love is hate, but I think it can be fear. Fear of abandonment, impermanence, or indifference will keep you from love. Love is grounding and makes you feel safe, and if you don't feel secure or felt threatened in the past, you'll suspect that everyone's out to get you. You'll be apprehensive about a boss, neighbors, new friends, even the plumber who fixes your pipes. (This is what I've seen happen to people who were bullied when they were kids—a lifetime of hesitation.) I think it's telling that when I suffered from anxiety, I was consumed by panic but was rarely afraid of other people or their motives because I was blessed with steady love from family and friends. Maybe Spirit also helped me instinctually feel the communal connection God talks about. Regardless, fear has nothing on love. I remember when Gram was dying, I was so afraid of living without her

> People think the opposite of love is hate, but I think it can be fear. Fear of abandonment, impermanence, or indifference will keep you from love.

advice, humor, and you know, even her French toast for dinner. What chased away my fear? The love I knew that was waiting for her in Heaven from Spirit. I know she was greeted by her brothers, sister, parents, and many friends.

Give Me Your Unconditional Love

Practicing and receiving love is crucial, but Spirit ups the ante when they say the primo love to give is unconditional love. So many times a soul's said to me, "I left the physical world not knowing what it was like to be unconditionally loved." And yet my knee-jerk reaction never changes: *What do you mean? Didn't you have grandparents? Or a pet?* Yet unconditional love isn't a given, and that's one of the most surprising things I've learned as a medium. It's easy to assume that people have similar experiences to you, especially with stuff you take for granted.

When I was upset that Gramps was in rehab, a nurse said to me, "One thing I can tell you is that your grandfather knows he is unconditionally loved. I guarantee it." She acted like this was rare, and when I looked around and saw how many patients had no visitors, I understood what she meant. I remember this craggy man named Henry staying down the hall, and how his family didn't see him as often as we saw Gramps, so my mom would bring him cigarettes and hot dogs. She didn't need to, but unconditional love comes naturally to Mom, and she really likes making others feel good. That woman has a lot of angel in her soul.

I usually think of love as a selfless act, and it is, but you do get something back from it. When actions stem from love, your soul feels lighter, and you feel proud of who you are. By definition, unconditional love doesn't have limits or restrictions, but Spirit says you won't benefit from having an entitled attitude about love either. You can't be a jerk and expect everyone to unconditionally love you the way you want. My friend Marie's in-laws are like this—they instigate rifts in their son's marriage and make passive-aggressive jabs in front of other relatives. However, they feel they deserve unconditional love, all the time and on demand, and it's hard for people to give it to them. In the end, nobody is happy—their children feel drained, and the parents have no friends. Giving some love isn't necessary to receive unconditional love, but it sure sweetens the exchange.

After a loved one dies, a lot of people still long for proof of unconditional love like a line from a journal or email, or—here's a shocker—

When actions stem from love, your soul feels lighter, and you feel proud of who you are.

a message from a medium. It's moving, then, when Spirit really delivers. When I was in Memphis, I read a man at my live show named Randy whose father, Arthur, died from throat cancer. Randy had told his wife, Dana, that afternoon that he thought mediums were dubious, eerie, and actually said, "What exactly does this lady do? Talk to dead people? Right!" Yet when Arthur's soul came through, the guy was all ears.

The first thing I said to him was, "Your dad wants to know what the hell you're doing here, talking to a lady who talks to dead people!" Spirit also told me Randy called me a "ghost whisperer," didn't want to attend the show, and was afraid of seeing familiar faces. Maybe that's why he freaked out when I told him I knew his nickname for me, his seats were coincidentally behind two friends, and his reading was projected onto a huge screen at the front of the theater, so everyone could see his reaction up close.

Right away, Arthur's soul validated his presence by talking about Randy's "new old car"—a 1978 Corvette Randy had just received from his own son for Father's Day. Tears streamed down Randy's face the minute I mentioned his father, as he nervously chewed gum at forty miles per hour. "Your dad wants you to know he rides with you in that car," I said, adding that Arthur was extremely proud of Randy and thought he was a great dad. This meant the world to Randy.

Throughout his life, Randy and his dad had a rocky relationship that stemmed from an inability to communicate their feelings. And although Randy and Dana took care of Arthur when he was sick, the two men remained emotionally distant. As a result, Randy always longed for the kind of father-son relationship other men he knew had, but never got his hopes up because they were always crushed. Arthur also never praised him for his hard work in school or life, though Randy was always a hard worker and now owns a very successful company.

Randy said the reading filled him with happiness and gratitude, and he was beside himself knowing that his father loved and valued him the way he'd always craved. And when Randy and his family ride in their Corvette now, Dana always holds the door open a little longer than usual and says, "Come on in, Arthur!" Randy says it creeps him out, but she knows he loves it. "He's no longer a skeptic and has a different take on the afterlife now," she told me. "When someone loses a loved one and says, 'I wish he or she could see me now,' Randy says, 'Oh believe me, they do!'" What's more, Randy's incredible story spread so fast through the city that Randy's phone rang off the hook the next day. "Everyone knew someone who told someone," Dana said. "So much for keeping it quiet!"

Don't wait until you're on the Other Side to spread such a positive vibe. Try to practice one act of unconditional love a day— big or small, for you or someone else. Run an errand for a flu-y friend or help a turtle cross the road. Anything goes, as long as it's entirely altruistic. At the end of my live shows, I explain that we can get so caught up in grieving the dead that we can forget about the living. I ask the audience to then turn to the person they came with, thank them for coming, and tell them how much they mean. After two hours of laughing and crying, the audience is ready to hug someone. You guys love love too.

Love Will Keep Us Together

When love is its most powerful, it does not stand alone. Love can be a starting point, a happy ending, or a series or revelations in between. Remember the deacon who said, "When you have faith, you have hope, and when you have hope, you have love"? Love is so transforming because it influences, and stands on the shoulders of, vital spiritual traits like faith, hope, generosity, compassion, grace, gratitude, and more. Just like we're connected to each other here and in Heaven, love can't be undone from our gifts and lessons because it's part of each one.

And when it comes to your intuition, the strongest love feeds it. In chapter thirteen, I talked about a young girl named Hannah who died from a brain tumor. Her mom, Sue, told me that Hannah and her little brother Robbie still have a special bond, although they're dimensions away. "She loved that boy with all her heart—he was her everything," Sue said. And since Hannah passed, Robbie sees and talks to her soul a lot. The day after her funeral, Robbie saw her standing in the street while he played on the swings, and months later, he looked at his bedroom window, pointed, and said to Sue, "Hannah's right there!"

It broke my heart to hear that Robbie told his mom that he wishes Hannah's stay in Heaven were only temporary. At only three and a half years old, he asked Sue, "Can Hannah come back yet? I miss her." So every evening, Sue reads him his favorite book, *Wherever You Are, My Love Will Find You*—which he calls "Hannah's book"—and knows that last page by heart: "you're my angel, my darling, my star, and my love will find you wherever you are." Then Sue always says, "And Hannah's love will find you wherever you are too." Robbie adores that ritual and gives her a huge smile before saying "Nite nite, Hannah" to the pictures he has of the two of them hanging above his bed.

During Hannah's eulogy, the hospital chaplain focused on the fact that Hannah's legacy was about the courage of her love—its ability to inspire and guide family and friends to love deeply and change the world. As the chaplain said, "Cancer never wins. Only love wins, over and over again." It also keeps us connected to those we love in Spirit, as Hannah and Robbie demonstrate every day.

When you make love a priority, Spirit does its best to replenish that feeling in their absence—whether it's by demonstrating that they're with you through signs or sending you others to fill their roles. During a live show in Toledo, Ohio, I read a woman named Cynthia whose daughter, Amber, and grandson, Jorgie, were horrifically killed by the baby's father. I'd actually read Cynthia at a show in Grand Rapids, Michigan, seven months earlier, and don't you know, Spirit guided me to her a second time. Cynthia was very close to her only daughter and felt joined at the hip with her, but she told me that Jorgie was truly "the love of [her] life" and her "best friend." It was no surprise to me, then, when I felt Amber's energy but found Jorgie's was the strongest in both readings.

Spirit told me they send Cynthia signs, and Jorgie's soul speaks to her. Cynthia kept Amber and Jorgie's pet dog, Roxie, and Jorgie's soul said he still interacts with Roxie on earth. This explains why Roxie, when swatting and barking by herself, looks like she has an invisible playmate! Another time, Cynthia passed her closet and a DVD randomly fell off a shelf and onto the floor—it was "Max & Ruby: Visit with Grandma," which she watched with Jorgie every day after daycare. And just before Jorgie was born, Cynthia couldn't wait to personalize the name "Grandma," and though she landed on "Me Me," Jorgie preferred "Mom Mom." Fast forward to two nights before Cynthia's first reading with me, when she heard Jorgie's voice in the middle of the night say, "Mom Mom!" No wonder Cynthia nearly fell off her chair when I asked her, "Your grandson talked to you the other night, didn't he?"

During Cynthia's second reading, Jorgie's soul showed me there were "new babies" in her life, and Amber's spirit said that Cynthia would have another chance to be surrounded by grandchildren. It came out that Cynthia's husband had newly reunited with his son from a prior relationship, and after a dinner, his son's daughter looked at Cynthia and yelled, "Me Me!" How strange, given the girl hardly knew Cynthia and this phrase was new to the toddler's parents. Amber was actually the only person who knew Cynthia had considered "Me Me" as a nickname! Spirit also told me the baby can see Amber's and Jorgie's souls, and I wouldn't be surprised if Amber helped bring these people into Cynthia's life to fill a void (similar to how a deceased wife's soul can guide her husband to his next marriage). Spirit doesn't think of it as being "replaced," but they know the type of love you miss and desire. True love has the ability to heal, transform, and transcend the deepest hurt, and they want you to have every chance to be happy again.

16

Forgive to Heal Yourself

It's not easy to forgive a person who's caused you pain, anger, or regret—be it a friend, family member, peer, or yourself. But no matter what the injustice, or whether it's a new or old wound, forgiveness is always in order. What a lot of people don't realize is that this gesture protects your own well-being, since it allows you to release bottled-up hurt and resentments. You're likely used to forgiveness that excuses a behavior for the other person's sake or because it's the right thing to do. But I feel forgiveness should aim to preserve your own self and soul, first.

You can see how you'd feel better if you cut yourself some slack, but how can forgiving others help you? Burdens are like emotional glue that keep you stuck to negative instances, feelings, and memories. So when you forgive a tormentor, you free yourself to heal. When a person betrays or wrongs you, don't think of forgiveness as a win for the perpetrator—*With my forgiveness, you get a clear conscience!*—but consider it an amazing gift to yourself, since you can start to heal by letting go. You'll stop being a victim and start feeling empowered again.

Act Now, Ask Questions La— Er, Never

Forgiveness usually comes with conditions that make you the passive recipient of feeling better. If you disappoint yourself, you might think, *I can't move past this until time heals my heart or I make it right.* But what does that even mean? Do you expect to wake up one morning and magically feel better? What if that day never comes or you stop trying to help yourself, because you begin to think you don't deserve forgiveness? None of these options makes you stronger or healthier.

Putting stipulations on forgiveness also gets you nowhere when you're waiting for someone else to make the first move. You might be like, *Once you apologize, then I'll forgive you.* But that's no good, because you remain bound to the person who harmed you and give them the power until they say, "I'm sorry." If they're not self-aware, don't soul-search, or, God forbid, die before they realize the extent to which they've upset you, guess who's out of luck? You, that's who.

Before you disagree, let's be clear about what forgiveness is and isn't. Forgiveness is not forgetting. It's not being a doormat. It's not a "get out of jail free" pass. Forgiveness is not an excuse to gloss over an issue or decide that the way you feel is not a big deal. It isn't condoning bad behavior or

> *Forgiveness is not forgetting. It's not being a doormat. It's not a "get out of jail free" pass.*

inviting a once-enemy to your home for Shabbat dinner. But what forgiveness is, is saying to yourself, "OK, that really stung. And I'm hurt. But it's time to take control of my feelings and future, and try to move past this already. I'm going to do that by forgiving the person responsible, even if the person is malicious, stupid, or me."

The longer you take to forgive, the more your anger will fuel negative emotions and revenge fantasies. This includes beating yourself up over things you feel you could have, should have, or would have done or said differently. I understand why this happens, since you may feel you have to reclaim control over the situation somehow. But holding grudges or even striking back is never the answer and rarely feels as gratifying as you'd think. The reason you're so upset is because you've been made to suffer—don't make it worse for yourself or do it to another person.

When you blow off forgiveness, you roll out the red carpet for negativity. You get stuck in the unhappiest parts of your life and never come back to who you truly are and what feels right. Know too that an unforgiving spirit affects everyone in your vicinity, since your moods help shape theirs. If you feel gross, it's easy to get annoyed with others. But if you feel good, you'll transfer that happiness, pay it forward, and teach those in your midst about forgiveness.

You're the keeper of your well-being, and forgiveness isn't about what's right and wrong. It's about what's right for you. If people are mean to you, I promise they're not thinking about how much they offended you or how awful you're feeling—at least not to the extent that you are or want them to be. And if you're mad at yourself, you're your own worst enemy when you let regret play on an endless loop in your head. I realize that hating yourself or another person gives you

If people are mean to you, I promise they're not thinking about how much they offended you or how awful you're feeling—at least not to the extent that you are or want them to be.

a place to put your hostility, but you don't need the consequences. Spirit wants you to turn the situation around with empathy, compassion, and self-protection.

Listen, a lot of people hurt you because they're hurting, and I'm not saying you shouldn't have some compassion for them. But you shouldn't have to constantly repair damage to your mind and soul because another person chooses to be sloppy or downright cruel with their words and/or behavior. I think a better option is to use forgiveness to protect yourself from a future need to heal, so you can control your reactions and feel less vulnerable around negative people.

So here's what I propose: unconditional forgiveness, which means forgiving first, before the other person asks for it or your own burdens drag you down. It works on any situation that warrants exoneration: a misunderstanding with an old friend, a stranger who cuts the line at the DMV, a jab from your brother-in-law about how you talk to your husband and kids. Unconditional forgiveness lets you move past all the pain and frustration, on your terms. It's about loving, honoring, and being kind to yourself—and as a result, having it in you to be good to others. Spirit says that not forgiving will eat away at an otherwise healthy soul.

So don't wait to confront your feelings or for another person to express theirs in a satisfying way. Unconditional forgiveness frees you now, so you can heal now. You can always call on your loved ones' souls for emotional backup.

Dear Me, I Forgive You. Love, Me

Departed loved ones are big advocates of self-forgiveness, because it forces you to put aside emotional self-flagellation and remember the good times you shared when they were alive. More than anything, their spirits plead for you to "please release the anger"; staying mad is like rubbing salt on self-inflicted wounds.

When you're upset with yourself, rage can send you running down unhealthy paths that distract you from finding a healing solution to your problems. But Spirit wants you to forgive the past, so you can enjoy what life is offering you right now. For a lot of my clients, that means honoring their loved one's memory in a positive way. Recently, I read a gentleman whose daughter died after he and his wife divorced. Spirit said he kept beating himself up about not being there more for his little girl, and prayed every night for God to take his soul so they could be together again. To encourage this to happen, he put himself in dangerous situations that could end his life. During the man's reading, his daughter's soul said to me, "My dad has to stop looking for trouble and doing stupid things to himself. Tell him to wear the hat!" I didn't know what this last part meant, but I did know that her soul protected her dad in situations where he otherwise should've been seriously harmed, since it wasn't his destiny to die yet. The man then explained that the "hat" Spirit referenced is actually a helmet he neglects to wear when he fools around on his motorcycle. His daughter's message hit him like a ton of bricks, though only he could

> *Forgive the past, so you can enjoy what life is offering you right now.*

decide to let go of his past, or else learn forgiveness when he dies. It's his choice to make the most of his time here or not.

When you hold on to old wounds, you actively elect to live in a funk. Spirit showed me your options as a landscape of hills and valleys, like at a ski resort. You can be on the top of a mountain, remembering good times with the sun on your face, or freeze your butt off in a wind tunnel of sadness below. So for that dad, he could embrace memories about Christmas morning or buying his daughter her first bike, and enjoy the signs he receives from Spirit, or weigh down his soul with why he used to work two jobs, went out with the guys after work all the time, and didn't live up to his own expectations as a father. I'm not sure what route he chose, but I am hoping it is the more positive one. Forgiveness is like the tram that'll zip him to the top of the mountain, but he has to buy a ticket.

OK, You're Forgiven Too

Spirit says you cannot change when a person hurts you, but unconditional forgiveness can help you alter the way you view that individual. When you forgive, you generally accept that people are flawed and more than their errors. They're human, like you and me. In fact, you know that famous Alexander Pope quote, "To err is human; to forgive, divine"? It reminds me of how Spirit says you harness the divine, or angelic, part of your soul when you forgive and see humanity for what it is. Listen, you've made mistakes and will continue to do so. Never forget what it's like to be the hurter—you're capable of inflicting wounds, just in different ways. You're not always the victim, is that correct?

If you think your life is hard, I've met people who've forgiven the unthinkable. During a live show in Dallas, I read a woman named Chrissy who has managed to forgive the man who shot and stabbed her twenty-one-year-old daughter, Heather. That would be Heather's boyfriend Brandon, who also killed Heather's stepmom, Lori. Brandon then left their two young children with the dead bodies for over six hours, until he anonymously called 911 to ask the police to check on his kids. When officers finally tracked Brandon down on the highway, he shot himself in the head. Another "coincidental" detail to this story is that Heather's final in-person conversation with her mother went like this: "Mom, you have to promise me you'll watch this show called *Long Island Medium.*" Chrissy agreed, obviously not knowing that the next time she'd hear from her daughter would be through me and from Heaven.

I mention all the gory details here because this play-by-play nightmare changed Chrissy's life forever. She's now raising her daughter's children, and during her reading, Spirit told me she'd forgiven the man who killed Heather and Lori. In fact, I saw that she prayed for his soul every night (yes, I just said that)! "I don't attend church every Sunday and can't remember the last time I opened a Bible," Chrissy told me. "But I do believe forgiveness is the right thing for myself and my grandbabies. How in the world can I teach them to love if I hold so much hate in my own heart?" What really blew me away was that Heather's soul brought Brandon's spirit forward to validate that they were together on the Other Side, albeit on different levels, and Chrissy was fine with it.

"I assume it was important for me to know she was with him, because someday I will tell her children what happened," she said. "I also believe part of why Heather did this was to put Brandon's mother at ease, because I talk to her often, since we share a common bond formed by tragedy and lean on each other for support." Chrissy feels that she lost a part of herself that day, but that God, her friends, family, and her daughter's spirit have helped her see that "life is still going and good can come from it." Her words, not mine. Now that's forgiveness.

Chrissy's healing process didn't happen overnight and is always evolving. When she initially lost her daughter, she said she felt "so alone, was so angry, hated life, hated everyone, and honestly believed that I had really pissed off God because why else would this happen to me?" Yet as time gradually passed, Chrissy clawed her way to forgiveness. Here's how she sums it up:

> *I had to allow my soul to take over my brain and feel thankful for what I had and not what I'd lost. Letting go of anger and resentment was the hardest thing I've ever done, but it was the biggest blessing I could ever encounter. A person cannot wake up one day and say they're no longer going to hate or be mad; it is a process, and it takes time and a lot of conversations within yourself. It is your mind talking to your soul, but once your soul takes over, you move on effortlessly. I know a lot of people have not forgiven Brandon, but I had to, because negative energy was consuming my life. When I forgave, a million weights lifted. Letting go is hard, forgiving is harder, but holding on to pain is hell.*

If there is a positive side to any of this, Chrissy said that knowing, firsthand, what the lesson of forgiveness feels like—"watching my world go from black to color again"—has helped her foster loving hearts in her grandkids. "The lesson my daughter's killer taught me, in a crazy way, was to forgive and love unconditionally," she said, "and that is a trait his children are learning from me." I also sense that on some level, Chrissy knows that unless she forgave Brandon, she'd remain handcuffed to him and the murder, and she didn't want to feel beholden to either.

Chrissy is living proof of a lesson I channel from Spirit all the time: forgiveness restores the soul and gives you back your life. You no longer focus on what could have happened, imagine how it should resolve, expect others to live in your reality, or beg for forgiveness. Hey, it takes strength. And all that hatred, suffering, grief, and loss doesn't immediately go away when you forgive someone, but you will work through it faster and begin to accept what occurred.

> *Forgiveness restores the soul and gives you back your life.*

Forgiveness Is a Powerful Teacher

There are so many lessons to learn from forgiveness that make your life happier and your soul lighter. When you forgive, you learn your capacity to give love and compassion against all odds. And while you might sympathize with someone whose aggression stems from their own pain, it's not important to understand where the suffering comes from to forgive it. But most of all, forgiveness lets you regain control of your feelings and your future. It helps you heal.

We're all in the physical world to make mistakes and accidentally hurt each other to some extent. If you were perfect, your soul would be in an angelic, Heavenly state. You need lots of different paths, in many lifetimes, to grow. You have to experience different cultures, races, heartaches, and joys. But because nobody's perfect, you have the capacity to be cruel, weak, confused, insensitive, grieving, needy, fragile, lost, selfish, and totally upside down. We are all souls on a journey that's filled with good and bad. And we are more alike than you think.

17

Grateful Is as Grateful Does

I'm down with having an "attitude of gratitude," so it's unfortunate that perky people suggest it when I'm in the worst mood, which makes me feel anything but thankful! They think it's the nice way to ask you to stop griping, when it should be a reminder that giving thanks brings happiness. And it does! In fact, after you've read this chapter, jot down a few things you're grateful for today. Then I'll see you back here in about two hours, because once you start listing, it's hard to stop. The more you express gratitude for what you have, the more you'll realize how much there is to feel grateful for. Including your do gooder friends!

Got Gratitude?

Spirit says gratitude is essential to happiness because it forces you to look at the overall picture of how many things are going right in your life. I'm not saying you should pretend pain and tragedy don't exist, but it's healthy to accentuate the positive sometimes. To feel gratitude, you have to optimistically survey your world from the outside in, which we don't do enough. And when you can express gratitude not just as an exercise but as a consistent way of being, you'll benefit.

Research backs me up on this. Various studies show that gratitude increases well-being and happiness, and is associated with having more energy, optimism, generosity, and empathy. Grateful people are also found to be less depressed, stressed, and more satisfied with their lives and relationships. They feel more in control of their purpose, growth, and self-acceptance, and I think I know why. When you're aware of what brings you joy, you're forced to acknowledge your blessings and consider where you are in life. From that positive, thoughtful perspective, you're able to see how purposeful and blessed your journey is.

Spirit says feeling and expressing gratitude also grows your soul and raises your vibration, because it's a major lesson we all need to learn. I think one reason that gratitude is a benchmark of spiritual development is that it can be really hard to feel it when life gets busy and haphazard. Like if you get a flat tire, it's a huge pain and can be dangerous, so your first instinct is to get pissed-off—it isn't to feel grateful for the stranger who fixes your tire for you, though this is what you might eventually admit. I also think that if you don't regularly acknowledge everything you have, society cues you to want more, which works against gratitude. But the more grateful you feel, the more aware you

> *The more grateful you feel, the more aware you are of all the gifts and blessings in your life.*

are of all the gifts and blessings in your life. You realize how the good balances out the bad.

How Do I Feel Grateful? Let Me Count the Ways . . .

Spirit wants you to feel glad for all the people and opportunities that influence you. Sure, you might be grateful for your family and friends, good health, a safe home, and a job that puts food on the table—maybe even the impulse that made you buy this book! Those are awesome but obvious examples. Think harder and more specifically, and you'll see that God's given you small, personalized gifts and blessings that are easy to overlook and take for granted. This might include having an organic juice bar in town that keeps your blood sugar up or a bank manager who gives your child lollipops and makes you feel like part of a community.

Try to get in the habit of recognizing the evident *and* less apparent stuff that brings you happiness on a regular basis. Doing this will shift your perspective toward seeing the positive, which is a great way to begin and end each day. I like to practice gratitude when the sun rises and sets, since it happens consistently and before/after you get sidetracked by commutes, carpools, and schedules. You can itemize all the things you appreciate, but you don't have to; a quick thanks is fine, like, "I'm grateful for another day to love and honor myself and my family." What Spirit doesn't want you to focus on is being pleased with material items. Enjoy them, sure, but don't dwell on them. You think God wants me to spend His time talking about my Christian Louboutin habit? I don't think so—not when I can raise my spirit by telling Him how appreciative I am that my family makes me laugh and how grateful

I like to practice gratitude when the sun rises and sets, since it happens consistently and before/after you get sidetracked by commutes, carpools, and schedules.

I feel to do His work in an entertaining and fulfilling way.

I can't tell you how many readings I've done where Spirit's said that we don't express enough gratitude toward each other while we're still alive. The souls of young people in particular like to say how grateful they are for their quality of life, especially if loved ones made them feel "normal" when they were sick. Read between the lines and you'll see that Spirit's emphasis is on how good we make each other feel, and how we take that gratitude with us into the afterlife because it's so valuable. But why wait until you're dead to tell your father, best friend, or even a sympathetic therapist how grateful you are for what they mean to you? It's so easy to do and can bring so much pleasure to you and the person hearing it.

Your loved ones' souls also tell me they appreciate when you go above and beyond for them. At a live show in Riverside, California, I read a woman named Dru whose firefighter husband, Rich, died from a sudden and unexpected brain aneurism. Shortly after they returned home from their honeymoon, Rich became ill from liver disease, and for ten more years, Dru cared for him until he passed away. That meant driving him to countless doctors, ER visits, surgeries, and specialists—sometimes going an hour each way to the facilities, up to three days a week. After receiving a liver transplant and living a healthy, medically regimented lifestyle, another frightening issue presented itself. Rich's kidneys began to fail, so Dru volunteered to give him one of hers. They'd just begun the screening process for Dru when, after a minor surgery for Rich to compensate for a small congenital heart valve issue, he collapsed and died the next day at home.

When I channeled Rich's soul, he and Dru experienced a moving reunion full of gratitude. Spirit validated its presence by mentioning their honeymoon in Hawaii, that Dru was wearing two pieces of jewelry he'd given her, and that she'd seen his spirit in her backyard (a few days before, Dru saw the shape of a person near a tree and felt Rich's soul while gardening). But what really mattered to Dru was that Rich finally thanked her for her devotion and care. He wanted her to know how much he valued the ways she nurtured him and that he thinks she is wonderful and deserves to be loved. His soul also told me that he chose to leave this world before she could give him her kidney, because he felt she'd already given him more than enough of herself. "It was so nice to hear from Rich that he appreciated me. Other people told me it was great how I took care of him, but I needed to hear it from him," Dru later said. "He was often grumpy from feeling sick and tired, so I had to practice patience a lot. It surprised me to hear his thanks and appreciation, and I didn't realize how much I needed it until I heard it."

Spirit says we get so caught up in our terrible moods, bad hair days, and countless errands that we forget how important we are to one another. I've talked about how we're all interconnected, but in terms of gratitude, you should also remember the domino effect that a gracious attitude has on everyone around you. Every moment of your day is part of a chain of events. Take this scenario, for instance. You wake up resenting your spouse for not unloading the dishwasher, which distracts him, so he leaves the house to go to the hardware store, where he knocks over a display, that falls on the owner, whose injury freaks out his wife. Or, you wake up grateful that your spouse usually unloads the dishwasher so you give him a pass this time, which makes him feel loved, so he cheers up the hardware store owner, who's in such a good mood that he brings his wife flowers.

See how that works? Spreading positivity like gratitude reminds me of that song my kids used to sing, "And the Green Grass Grows All Around," which is about the interdependence of a bug, bird, and tree. I read online that this is called a cumulative song, which is where the first line of each verse introduces a new item until there's a list of them that makes up the tune and its story. "The Twelve Days of Christmas" is another example in this genre, with its countdown of leaping lords, dancing ladies, milking maids . . . you know the rest. Anyway, our lives remind me of a cumulative song too, in that all your actions build on each other to shape the world around you. When we consider how you affect every piece of the puzzle, you can see how everyone benefits when you feel grateful.

Gratitude Breeds Goodness

Gratitude is an emotion you feel, but I think it's also a visceral form of guidance, because, like Spirit, it instinctively encourages you to consider how special life is and helps you to positively focus on what you have and not what you lack. People can say, "I'm thankful for this, I'm blessed for that" until they're

> To be truly grateful isn't just a statement— it's a way of life.

blue in the face, but to be truly grateful isn't just a statement—it's a way of life. My parents taught me that actions speak louder than words, and Spirit says that gratitude will help motivate you to act with more empathy, generosity, kindness, and thoughtfulness.

God, your soul, and all Spirit, really, are grateful when you participate in acts of goodness, especially service. You might want to occasionally check in with yourself about whether you're contributing to the greater good. You don't have to wonder if every minute of your life benefits others, but pay attention to how your gut responds to your daily routine. Goodness should feel good.

Oh, and don't do the right thing because you think it'll help you get past the pearly gates. You think I bust my rear talking to dead people so I can get into Heaven? That's not how Spirit says it works. It's more like, God gave you life, so your gift to God is your actions. He's the big teacher, and you want to make your teacher proud. Spirit wants you to do things because you want to, not because there's something in it for you. But if you commit to the highest good, what you end up wanting to do will ultimately please God! And if your actions are sincere, your soul will grow—there's the afterlife perk. An evolved soul is partly the result of good intentions, not a means to an end or the reason for having them at all.

Even if you don't have a lot of time to do good, that's fine. Small efforts can add up to a sizable contribution, and I'm not just talking charity or volunteer work. Random acts of kindness and favors count as service, like driving an elderly friend to the doctor's or shoveling a neighbor's driveway without him asking. There's a florist in Manhattan named Bella Meyer who's said that inspiring others to smile, or bring a moment's peace, is a source of happiness and fascination for her. So on the rainiest, cloudiest, and most miserable days, when people need a little more joy than usual, she and a team of coworkers and volunteers hit the subways and streets to hand out free flowers that bring happiness. Bella looks for the crankiest folks she can find. She smiles, makes eye contact, and then makes people's days with her vibrant gifts.

In the end, it doesn't matter if you volunteer or get paid to do for others; when you see a person's face light up or hear how thankful they are, everyone benefits, because you also feel grateful for a glimpse at the angel in yourself. Have you ever noticed the amazing surge of energy you feel after acting kind or helpful? That's your soul's way of saying, "Hooray! Job well done."

18

Come On, Get Happy

One of the biggest lessons I've learned from Spirit is that they want you to experience as much happiness as you can in this lifetime, and that the stuff that brings you joy is very personal. It can even seem ordinary to others. I might feel on top of the world singin' and dancin' to Pharrell's hit song "Happy," but you might be thrilled to just eat Chinese again, since the thought of chicken lo mein made you cry your eyes out since Aunt Lulu died (it was her favorite).

However you seek happiness, Spirit says to chase it hard and use it well, because the rewards are great. The happy people I meet are kind, loving, forgiving, caring, and altruistic. They're hip to the benefits of a pleasant attitude, so they choose happiness and don't wait for it to find them. They make the most of every moment, and when they're in a rough stretch, they celebrate small pleasures when they can. God doesn't want you to trudge through life, learning all these demanding lessons, just to celebrate when you're in

Heaven! What Spirit teaches will grow your soul, but it also drives you toward a more positive experience here.

If You're Happy and You Know It . . .

Some think happiness happens to you, but Spirit says you have to pursue it to a certain extent. Playing tag with your fiancé in a spring rain shower or pausing to watch a family of ducks cross the road might bring you unexpected bliss, but you still have to do something to enjoy it—get outside, take a beat, and embrace the moment. You have to accept happiness from the people and opportunities that offer it.

Spirit says feeling happy requires a conscious choice to start activities with optimism and self-confidence. Happiness doesn't just fall in your lap. It's also not about waking up one day and deciding to be happy, but framing situations with positivity and assurance that if your plans go south, there's a reason. In other words, happiness doesn't depend on what happens but on how you perceive what happens. It's like if you're single and see the same woman every morning on your walk to work. If she's hot, you think it's meant to be; if she's not, you think it's a shitty coincidence and she's stalking you! Same situation, different perspective.

Seeing things in a positive light is an ongoing decision—you may have to remind yourself to handle situations in a pleasing way. A lot of my clients think happiness starts when a friend makes them laugh, a date makes them dinner, or they connect with a loved one's soul for closure via a medium. But I tell every person I read or come in contact with, "Plenty of things can make you happy, but they aren't responsible for your happiness. You are." Am I right, or am I right?

A big part of being happy is truly believing that Spirit is there for support—that God, your guides, souls of faith, angels, and loved ones are ready to help if you call on them. Rather than fight or grumble about what can't be changed, Spirit says to accept what's going on and use your energy to deal with the situation as it is. And when you look for backup from people in the physical world, be sure they're realistic, positive, and good listeners. I think about health-related online message boards, especially the ones that deal with hard-to-diagnose conditions like chronic pain. And they're always colored with negative complaints and sadness. Meanwhile, if you go to a message board for the same condition that's related to a treatment solution, like nutrition, it's so upbeat and full of life! The happy people are dealing with the situation as it exists—not how they feel it should be or wish it were. They don't see themselves as victims, and the attitude shift makes them hopeful. Besides, I think Spirit's at their best when you're ready to make positive changes while enlisting their help. They remind me of Tom Cruise in *Jerry Maguire* when he says, "Help me, help you!"—minus the slick grin.

Because Spirit loves to see you happy, they're with you at your most thrilling moments—weddings, graduations, birthdays, and the like. When I was in Toronto,

> *Spirit's at their best when you're ready to make positive changes while enlisting their help. They remind me of Tom Cruise in Jerry Maguire when he says, "Help me, help you!"*

I read a young woman named Natalie whose father died in an accident when she was five years old. After getting engaged, she couldn't imagine how she was going to get married without her dad there, but his soul came through to give his blessing. He said that her fiancé, Mark, is a gentleman and gave him permission to marry her. This is especially sweet, because Mark visited the dad's tombstone and asked, in his head, for his approval to propose; Natalie said the day was cloudy and dark, but as Mark left, he saw a break of sun and felt it was a sign. Her father's soul also asked me to tell Natalie to make her big day a happy one and not to focus on missing him, since Spirit will be with her when she walks down the aisle. "I've learned not to stay stuck in the past when my loved ones' souls are with me," she said. "I won't let life pass me by or feel guilty about my happiness."

Spirit also wants you to be careful about who you hold close, because happiness depends on it. If you spend time in relationships that make you upset, you'll absorb negativity like a sponge. You'll pass it on and maybe even get sick from it. But when you surround yourself with support, good energy is limitless.

I don't think it's your responsibility to help nasty people increase their happiness all the time, but if you're happy, that's one of the best ways to affect their attitudes. A warm smile or a hand on a shoulder cuts across every age, language, and mood barrier. It reminds me of how my girlfriend Jen was at Whole Foods the other day, and a man held the glass door open

> *Be careful about who you hold close, because your happiness depends on it. If you spend time in relationships that make you upset, you'll absorb negativity like a sponge.*

to the pastry case when she reached for a muffin. Without thinking, she said, "That's so kind, thank you"—and the guy's jaw dropped open. He was like, "Ma'am, thank *you* for acknowledging it!" That's right, he thanked Jen for thanking him. Judging by this guy's reaction, grateful gestures don't happen to him enough!

Don't Be a Happiness Commitment-Phobe

I'm no doctor, but I've been known to diagnose my clients with a case of the "when's." These are the folks that say, "Theresa, I know I'll be happy when . . ." and then name an expectation: get married, have a baby, find a new job, retire—basically, when they get past what they think is holding them back from happiness. But get this: Spirit says that filling in the blank rarely makes people as happy as they expect, because each new situation opens the door to potential conflict. That's life! Take relationships, for example. You may think you'll be happy when you meet your soul mate, but that person comes with baggage and demands on your time. Or with a new car, you might have more expensive insurance or complicated tune-ups.

So what's my prescription for the "when's"? I tell people that happiness is up for grabs now, only you can make yourself feel it, and to own the choices that add to and subtract from your bliss. Read that sentence twice, then don't call me in the morning, because I'll be busy drinking my coffee.

Spirit says it helps to make a commitment to happiness. I don't mean that you need to be positive against all odds, or obligated to feign pleasure when it's unnatural. But you should vow to yourself that you'll find some good to lighten the load when you need it.

Committing to happiness shouldn't feel like a duty or chore either, since all you're really doing is making a pledge to be good to yourself. It's no different in a job, when you make a commitment to your boss, or when you have a family and commit to your spouse and kids. Spirit wants you to be dedicated and faithful when navigating life's challenges. You're making a promise to your soul that you'll do the best you can on the path it chose.

To be honest, I think finding happiness "now" is easier than "when." As you know, I don't like waiting for things to happen, and "now" doesn't try my patience. I also like to benefit from traits that encourage happiness, like gratitude, forgiveness, love, and kindness. So how do you know when you're happy? It seems like an obvious answer, and most people think that the signs will shout at them, like a huge emotional rush or burst of laughter. But for me, long-term happiness feels more like a steady contentedness. It's going through the day without needing to ask "Why?" because you already trust there's a reason. And if you feel your happiness dipping, you also know it's OK to treat yourself; getting my hair done or buying a great pair of slippers at Target always makes me smile. Besides, if you told me you were ecstatic 24/7, I'd think you were lying or on heavy meds. Feeling constantly euphoric in the physical world isn't realistic or sane!

As you know, Spirit doesn't want us to be happy just so we can feel good—it's to affect others too. When you're happy, you have a little more *zip-a-dee-doo-dah* to share with everyone around you, whether it's in the form of time, money, advice, patience, or an encouraging pat on the back. And when you're wrestling with grief, one of the main reasons Spirit wants you to embrace happiness is so others can get back to theirs. Once I read an anguished mother named Stacy whose daughter Kaylee, at the age of eleven months, died from a rare mitochondrial genetic disorder. "I carry so much guilt because I loved her so much and would have done anything to save her, though as much as we tried, we couldn't," Stacy shared. No wonder Kaylee's soul told me her dad prays to her to help Stacy find peace and happiness again. Her father validated this, and Stacy felt the message was Kaylee's way of saying Stacy's going to be OK and that Kaylee's looking out for her. "She wants me to be happy and live," she said.

Happiness Can Be Harder Than Acrylic Nail Tips

No matter how challenging or unfair your life feels in the physical world, please know that Heaven is a happy place. Spirit tells me that when you pass, you're greeted by the souls of familiar faces during a wonderful reunion. You feel peaceful, safe, cherished, and intimately connected to God's love. There is no judgment, blame, envy, fear, ego, anger, or other destructive emotions to speak of. There's also no suffering on the Other Side, souls move freely, and all pain is left in the physical world with the human body. Coincidentally, most near-death experience survivors tell similar stories about how Spirit sings, dances, and plays with animals in a technicolor landscape full of gemstones, beautiful music, and crystal waterfalls. Add a spinning ballerina, and being on the Other Side sounds a lot like living in the perfect jewelry box.

Spirit also tells me your soul feels "fulfilled" in Heaven, because you've completed your journey, despite various roadblocks. But while learning lessons can feel difficult at times, they become impossible if you're unhappy.

Optimists, however, react to problems with a sense of confidence and belief in the ability to tackle the task at hand. They think negative events are temporary and don't saturate every aspect of a person's life. I've found that optimists also choose to remember the good when it comes to grief. Every November a friend who lost her grandma within days of my Gram's passing texts me to bemoan the holidays. She'll go on about what a sad time of year it is, but I can never relate because I'm an innate optimist. When I hear Bing Crosby or smell cookies like Gram and I used to bake, I actually get a warm feeling and my mind goes to happy memories, not sad ones. I remember decorating the tree, playing cards after dinner, and teasing Gram about how she made the wrong sauce for her cauliflower. When happy people can't change the event that makes them blue, they change the way they react to it. I obviously can't alter the fact that Gram died, but I can choose to remember her in a positive way that fills me with delight.

A lot of times we hold on to negative emotions, let them fester, and before we know it, we've made a mountain out of a molehill. Spirit warns against this a lot, and my sign for it is the face of a client named Sammy. When I met him, he hadn't talked to his sister in six years and both his parents had died. His mom's soul asked him to reevaluate the situation with his sibling, since the two couldn't even remember why they weren't speaking. When I saw Sammy the next year, he told me he'd rekindled the relationship and it was better than ever. Spirit doesn't want you to have toxic people in your life, but when there's a trivial rift, they will step in because no misunderstanding should get in the way of healing and building relationships. Those are two important topics that weave through your lessons.

When you're suffering, Spirit insists that the fastest way to sink even further is by comparing yourself to others. We are always better than somebody we know in some way, and you always want what you can't have. When you have curly hair, you want straight hair; when you have short hair, you want long.

But when you evaluate who you are, side by side with others, they never excel in every category, so why wish you were them? Your friend who has a great relationship with her mom might not have such a good thing with her spouse. Or maybe you envy your sister who's still married, because your husband died young from cancer. But would you also want her inability to hold down a job? Listen, a person's life is more than one thing. Spirit says you have to be happy with yourself, and if you let someone else make you feel bad, it's your own fault. For this, they'll show me how I never felt pretty or thin enough as a young woman, and ask me to share how I feel now—happy, successful, comfortable in my skin, and loving a few snug dresses. I choose to accept who I am and no longer judge myself according to a narrow and inaccurate view of who others seem to be.

Happiness is ours for the taking, but we have to really want it. Spirit would never tempt you with such an incredible gift if you weren't meant to embrace it.

19

Let Go of Guilt, Shame, and Regrets

No matter how strong or resilient you are, guilt, shame, and regret are negative emotions we've all dealt with at one time. Whether it comes from eating that third piece of pie on Thanksgiving, talking smack about a relative, or processing the loss of a loved one, this trifecta is a fast track to unhappy thoughts and a hampered soul. But because Spirit is always with you, loving and guiding you from the Other Side, they want you to take a closer look at the burdens that weigh on you. While guilt and regret might be considered "helpful" in some cases, it's a problem when their impact loads down your soul. Spirit's told me that this kind of negativity serves no constructive purpose here or in the afterlife, other than that it's a challenge you may need to overcome while learning lessons. No wonder Spirit always insists that you let go of guilt, shame, and regrets; it's impossible to embrace life the way God wants and your soul needs, when you hold on to them!

Meet The Tricky Trio

I refer to guilt, shame, and regret as the Tricky Trio because we tend to feel them together or as a result of one another, though you can experience one without the others too. Also keep in mind that the way I understand these terms are as Spirit explains them to me, which is as they relate to your happiness here and in Heaven. I'm sure psychologists and philosophers parse them out differently, since I don't think they're getting their information from dead people and the divine!

Spirit tells me that guilt is a deeply felt emotion that comes from something you've done; think of it as remorse for a wrong-doing, whether that fault is real or imagined. If guilt had a punishing sister, it would be shame, which is more personal and relates to feeling bad about who you are. So whereas guilt deals with specific behaviors, shame is what you feel when you question your worth; in fact, it can come from feeling guilty. Regret, then, is the fallout of either or both of these emotions—it's how miserable, sorry, and disappointed you feel about an event or the way a person acted. You might also feel regret for an action or feeling that didn't happen, but that you wish had (for instance, if you regret never telling your dad how much you loved him). If that's not hard enough, the Tricky Trio can also be linked to embarrassment, annoyance, anxiety, and depression.

Although Spirit mostly addresses harmful guilt, shame, and regret, since their intention is to help you heal from negative feelings, sometimes the Tricky Trio can be useful. These three feelings might help you know when to admit you're wrong or change your behavior for the better; they can also lead to personal growth and social change. The hard thing is, both good and bad types of guilt and regret feel the same, so you can't simply react to these emotions without thinking first. Spirit's lesson, then, isn't about learning when it's OK to make mistakes or get things wrong, but how to deal with the Tricky Trio when it strikes. Nobody's perfect, but if you've made a choice that leads to these emotions, Spirit suggests you acknowledge the shortcoming, grieve it if necessary, then let it go. I'm not saying your actions don't matter, because they do—your choices affect future decisions and growth. But Spirit says there's always room for improvement, not just here but in future lifetimes, if you do fall short. This makes holding on to guilt, shame, and regret in the physical world pointless and damaging.

Spirit never ceases to amaze me, especially when they frame negative emotions like guilt, shame, and regret in a positive way so that it's easier to digest their messages and lessons. This means that while your loved ones may use the word "guilt," they never talk about "shame" or break down your "regrets" too deeply, because these two feelings can feel heavy and burdensome. Instead, when addressing the topic of shame, they'll show me the soul pulling a baseball cap over its eyes, which is my symbol for when Spirit isn't proud of how it handled certain situations in the physical world and is offering an apology. But it's done in such a coy and sweet way! And when Spirit addresses your regrets or theirs, they phrase all misgivings in a careful and earnest manner, which I'll get into later.

Since we're talking language related to the Tricky Trio, Spirit also doesn't use the word "mistake" with me, but instead will explain how a poor decision can become a teaching moment. Because we live in such a justice-based society, a lot of us think that

> *So many of our wise choices are overshadowed by not-so-great ones, yet the big reason you're here is to learn from the good and bad.*

if you make an error, it has to become who you are as a person and should follow you around forever. No wonder humans carry so much shame! So many of our wise choices are overshadowed by not-so-great ones, yet the big reason you're here is to learn from the good and bad. So rather than let you hold yourself in contempt over a "mistake," Spirit will encourage you to make better decisions next time. Their angle reminds me of how you revisit botched or unlearned lessons in future lifetimes or study them in Heaven; I'm told there's no punishing consequence if you're a slow learner. You just try again. If you think about it, a lot of what you're doing right now is a second chance, since some of the lessons you're learning in this life are ones you've flubbed up before.

Guilt and Shame Are in Your Head, Not Your Gut

The important thing to realize about guilt and shame is that they're learned feelings. Throughout your life, you gather different values that feel right and use them to define your morality. These morals are intended to make life more meaningful and give you a healthy sense

> *A lot of what you're doing right now is a second chance, since some of the lessons you're learning in this life are ones you've flubbed up before.*

of right and wrong. Maybe they're influenced by parents, religion, friends, life-changing events, or any combination of factors that ultimately impact how you react to situations the way you do.

Spirit shows me that these morals can become a little, well, let's say "misguided," when you use them to judge and beat yourself up, which can cause shame. Humiliation or disgrace isn't part of morality; it's how you've chosen to use it. Look at kids! They don't have guilt or shame until adults teach them how and when to feel it. The only emotion kids feel after stealing a cookie or drawing on walls is one of awesomeness! Growing up, some of you learned how to feel guilt, shame, and regret a little too well, which causes you to assume that when you feel any guilt at all, you deserve punishment and judgment—from yourself, others, God . . . stop me anytime. A moral compass is necessary for telling you when to apologize for hurting a friend or how to stop repeating bad habits, but if your immediate reaction to feeling bad is always guilt, you're going to spend a lot of unnecessary time in a dark and self-defeating frame of mind.

So the next time you default to guilt or shame, no matter how warranted you may feel it is, Spirit wants you to stop, truly consider what's happened, then approach the way you feel with mindfulness and perspective. Reflecting on a situation will let you react appropriately, zero in on what's draining your positive energy, learn from the situation, and then release the burden or make a change.

When you turn your guilt inward, causing shame, you accept that you are your mistake—and that's just not true. Survivor's guilt can cause shame too, and it comes up a lot during readings because Spirit doesn't want it to weigh on your soul. In my frame of reference, survivor's guilt is when people think they did something wrong because they survived a traumatic accident and the other person did not. For me, this comes up a lot with war, natural disasters, cancers, organ donations, and car accidents—but anyone can feel survivor's guilt when a loved one dies. I think one reason survivor's guilt is so common is because it's easier to blame someone for what happened than to accept and deal with what it means when a loved one has exited your life. It's simpler than facing a complicated reality.

When you turn your guilt inward, causing shame, you accept that you are your mistake—and that's just not true.

Guilt and shame can feel heaviest when you misinterpret how you affect others' feelings. Let's say you accidentally run over your neighbor's prize roses backing out of the driveway. You feel like a schmuck, so you offer to replace them and think it's a fair suggestion. Done, moving on. But then your neighbor tells you he's furious and heartbroken, and this makes you feel so much worse. Now you swing into guilt, shame, and regret mode. You swear you're a horrible driver, a jerk for being so flippant about an old man's flowers, remorseful that you didn't also buy him a butterfly bush . . . *Can you ever look him in the eye again!?* Good grief, enough already. See how the Tricky Trio flies out of control?

Listen, Spirit says you can't cause emotional pain to another person. You can trigger emotional pain, but people's angst comes from inside of them, not from you. The neighbor in this story could just as easily prefer to see his crushed roses in a favorable light: he gets to plant a new garden now, maybe try different flowers, and should probably thank you for footing the bill too. You did the right thing. The fact that he's devastated beyond reason is his choice.

All of this is to say that guilt and shame are a frame of mind. Unhappiness comes from thinking you don't deserve it; the situation itself doesn't say that! So make sure that when you feel guilt, you know where it's coming from and that you process it productively. If your guilt is legit, don't define yourself by it; work through it, put it to good use if you can, and then release it. Remember, guilt can be healthy if it's put to positive use. If you feel guilty after yet another one-night stand, think of it as your soul telling you that you were raised better than that. But if you feel guilty taking a long lunch on a gorgeous day, then this may be a sign that you feel unnecessarily bad when you're good to yourself, and that needs some attention. Spirit wants you to make choices that nourish your soul, not punish it.

Make choices that nourish your soul, not punish it.

Again, Spirit says guilt and shame are decisions. Suffering comes from thinking life is horrible rather than it actually being horrible. If you choose to lug around guilt and shame, then it stands to reason that you choose to live in the past and remain in a negative huff. Why not free yourself from those burdens?

Living and Channeling with "No Regrets"

Spirit says regret happens when you feel sorry or ashamed about how a situation unfolds. I hear this a lot from clients and loved ones in Spirit—a wife who regrets not looking for more signs since her spouse died, a mom who regrets not bringing a child home to pass with her family around, a father's soul who regrets coming down too hard on his son when he was a little boy. I also find that regrets are more often expressed by people who've passed later in life than they are by children's departed souls. I'm not sure if this has to do with the fact that youthful souls are less flawed or that as we get older we have more time to rack up regrets, but during a reading, those who die young seem to focus more on happy memories than apologies and remorse.

And as with shame, Spirit frames its own regrets so they go down easy. Your loved ones' souls rarely say to me "I regret . . . ," but they do say "I've learned a lesson on the Other Side about . . . ," "I wish I'd told you more . . . ," or "I'm sorry that . . ." This turns a potentially melancholy tone into a pure, enlightened, and rather angelic one. They might also try to reduce *your* regrets. When I read a gentleman in Williamsport, Pennsylvania, who'd lost his wife, her soul said to me, "Please tell my husband that I know how much he misses me and that he never thought he'd miss me this much. He keeps saying, 'I wish I'd spent more time with her,' but tell him to stop doing that! I know how deeply he cared."

Imagine if you approached regret the way Spirit does every day. What if you thanked people for what they've taught you, shared how sorry you are for hurting them, and told them how you feel—before leaving them? Would you have fewer regrets in the physical world and after? Of course you would. I don't think it's possible to live on this plane without *any* regrets, but you sure would feel better about yourself, which might even eliminate shame altogether.

Some of the most amazing souls I've channeled have made "no

regrets" their motto in the physical world, including one of the craziest readings I've ever done. Here I channeled Talia Joy, an Internet celebrity known for her YouTube channel "TaliaJoy18." Talia was thirteen years old when she died after fighting neuroblastoma, a rare pediatric cancer. When Talia was first diagnosed, she began putting on makeup to feel pretty because she'd lost her hair from chemo—it was her way of drawing less attention to her bald head. So she dedicated her YouTube channel to incredible makeup tutorials, fashion, and cancer vlogs, and her inspiring strength and optimistic attitude quickly made her famous. She appeared on *The Ellen DeGeneres Show* and was made an honorary face for Cover-Girl cosmetics, appearing in their ads with the self-confident tagline "Makeup is my wig." However, Talia was perhaps most famous for working through a fun bucket list of goals, including "give flowers to a stranger," "make my own lipstick," "have a cake fight," and #61—"Go to a *Long Island Medium* show."

I heard about Talia's bucket list on a Friday and felt a strong, intuitive pull to meet her. To be honest, I had no clue who Talia Joy was, but all I had to hear was that she had cancer, used makeup as her wig—and forget it, I was as good as there. I also didn't know how sick Talia was at the time, but my instincts told me to see her very soon. On Monday afternoon, I decided, with no hesitations, to fly out the next morning. I remember saying to myself, "Please don't die while I'm there. I don't think I'm strong enough to be part of that beautiful girl's passing." I shut down production for the show, which I've never done before, and though I planned to fly out around eight a.m., a scheduling issue put me on an eleven a.m. flight. When Talia heard I was coming, her mother, Desiree, said she smiled and felt happy despite the pain she was in. But once I landed in Florida, where she lived, I checked my phone and saw a message from my manager. Talia had died at 11:22 a.m. that morning, shortly after I took off (it's an angelic number sequence too).

This is when I freaked the freak out. First of all, I felt incredibly guilty for hoping Talia didn't pass when I was by her side. Did I cause this? No, that couldn't be. Plus, I wasn't sure what to do next—go to the hospital? Let her family grieve in peace? I decided to go, because I knew God put me on that plane for a reason. So I stopped in the bathroom, on the verge of tears and a breakdown, and as I peed, I said to Spirit, "I don't know if this is the right thing to do." Just then I heard, "Theresa, thank you for coming. You are the last gift from me to my mother." It was Talia's soul! Talking to me on the toilet! If that weren't insane enough, I then left the stall and as I was washing my hands, a random twelve-year-old girl ran up to me and said, "Oh my God, you're the Long Island Medium! My name is Talia, and my mom and I watch your show all the time!"

"*What did you say?!*" I basically shouted at her. "Do you know that Talia Joy just died, and you're telling me your name is Talia, and I've never even heard that name before?! Do you understand how insane that is?!" Afterward I thought, *I should've taken a photo with that girl, because nobody will believe this story.*

When I arrived at the hospital, Talia's body was still in the room. I didn't want to overstep my boundaries so I lingered uneasily and expressed my condolences. That's when I realized Talia's soul had left her body and was actually behind me.

"Theresa, they're going to take my body soon," her soul said. "I'd like some alone time with my mom. Can you tell everyone that?" So I carefully shared the message, and as Talia's family and friends left the room, Talia's mom, Desiree, asked me to stay. I hung around for a bit, but wanted to leave Desiree with her daughter, as Talia asked; if God sent me there to just give her mother this final moment, the trip would've been worth it. After Talia's body was removed, I came back to sit with Desiree and Talia's oldest sister, Mattia, to channel Talia's soul.

"Do I have to have hair on the Other Side?"—that was one of Talia's first questions to me! And I told her soul, "You don't." You can take on any look you want in Heaven. Because Talia was proud of the smooth head that redefined beauty for girls all over the world, she stayed just as she was in the physical world.

Talia's energy was so strong that it was clear that she is a very evolved soul. First off, I felt like she was actually in the room having a conversation with me—she didn't send me signs and symbols, like when I usually work. Because Spirit uses my physical body when I channel, I also felt Talia's bubbly, happy energy in such an all-encompassing way that it was a bit awkward for me—here I am in a room full of mourners, and Talia has me jumping up and down, like, "Oh my God, I can't believe you're here!" Her soul also had to have known she would pass, and when, and that I would be the last person she saw. Talia's bucket list had seventy-four items on it, and on the day she died, she didn't plan to meet Pink or Usher—she met a medium who ultimately helped her speak to her family from Heaven. I really feel that decision was made with her soul. I suspect too that Talia's wisdom in life was that of an old soul—Desiree said Talia often told her, calmly, that she'd be OK and could handle whatever God gave her. She sure did.

Apparently a spiritual healer sat with Talia the weekend before she passed and said, "Something amazing is going to happen on Tuesday." When Desiree told me that story, she said, "It was you!" But I corrected her: "No, it was Talia being free of pain and her soul going to Heaven." I know Talia's happy on the Other Side. Her soul said she's a greeter of children who cross over. God often chooses youthful souls to transition kids to Heaven by showing them the ropes—it's like, "Hey, I was also young, and I'm OK. You can still do all the things you love to do on earth." Talia makes children feel special and fearless by doing their makeup.

I wanted to put Talia's fascinating story in this chapter about regrets because so much of her legacy was about not having them. I feel this must have been a major lesson for her to learn here, and she did so with flying colors. The "evidence" is clear to me: One of Talia's mantras was "No regrets." Talia's beauty platform was about never feeling shame or apologizing for who you are. The reason Talia created a bucket list was so she wouldn't have regrets before she passed. Talia's death was even a lesson for me about not feeling guilt about her dying while I was in-flight, or regret about channeling her at a time that might have seemed too sensitive or inappropriate for her family. I think God was reminding me that my purpose is to connect souls with loved ones here and that my personal fears are secondary. When Spirit calls me to channel, there is never a "bad time."

Talia's soul asked her family not to feel guilt or have regrets, as well. She said she had "no regrets" about her passing, which weighed heavily on Desiree's mind. "I do not want anyone to go over anything that should have been different because Mom, the only thing [worth changing is that I'd have lived, and it was my destiny to go]," Talia had me say. "Everything else was perfect. You made all my wishes come true." Her soul also encouraged Mattia to live each day to the fullest, and not to dwell on any fears about her own health or that of her future children, and to stop going over memories that make her "feel bad or sad." In other words, she gave her sister every reason to avoid guilt or regret in a future without her.

All Talia's soul asked was for her legacy to go on among family, friends, and fans, including the completion of her bucket list and continuation of her YouTube channel. Desiree has done this, plus gone above and beyond by launching a nonprofit that raises money for clinical trials and research in childhood cancer, and working closely with CoverGirl to host makeover classes for young women battling cancer, among other efforts. Talia's overwhelming lesson to her family, and us, is to embrace every moment and opportunity in life, and to know that she's with us, embracing it too. No guilt, no shame, no regrets.

As Elsa Might Say, "Let It Go!"

Spirit never tells people to "move on," but they do want you to carry on. Otherwise it will feel impossible to progress emotionally, spiritually, and physically. Negativity can break down moods, distort your perception, cause doubt, and harm health. It even gets in the way of completing goals, because all of your choices are made under a black cloud. I

> *Spirit never tells people to "move on," but they do want you to carry on. Otherwise it will feel impossible to progress emotionally, spiritually, and physically.*

don't look so hot in that light, do you? You don't have to forget your sadness or tragedy, but you may want to make it a goal to start each day with a pleasant attitude, reach out to those who support you, and do what you can to feel happy, healthy, and functional.

Spirit needs you to know it's necessary to move past negative burdens, but especially heartache. The upsides of this intention may seem obvious, but when grief is the most recent reminder of how a loved one makes you feel about them, you might hesitate to let go of this emotion too. When I was in Phoenix, I read a family whose sixteen-month-old son, Sage, died in a dreadful accident. The gang was headed to the gym, and as Sage's father, Jake, loaded his three sons into the car, Sage ran out of the garage and after his grandpa, who was driving away and—here it comes—accidentally ran him over. Grandpa didn't see Sage dart out, and sadly, Jake was too far from Sage for anything to be stopped. Sage's grandfather immediately called 911, and a helicopter flew Sage to the hospital. Since then, a deep and unrelenting sorrow had been crushing the family, particularly Jake.

During the reading, Spirit got to work at helping this family carry on from their loss. Sage's soul assured me that when he passed, he died in his father's arms after the accident and not in the helicopter transporting him to the hospital, as a nurse later assumed and told his family. Sage felt no pain. And while Jake has struggled with a lot of guilt since his son died, Spirit said it was not his fault and asked him to release it. Sage's soul assured his family that it was his destiny to pass, so Jake could not have protected him. Jake also felt guilt for not kissing Sage before he left for work that morning, like he did every day. "Listen, he still feels the love you give him as a family," I told them. Sage's soul told me that kissing or not kissing him wouldn't have changed how much he knows his dad loves him.

Ultimately, Sage's message helped Jake accept the accident and reconcile his guilt and regrets. It also taught the family about acceptance and letting go—"not letting go of Sage or the memories we have, but the time we still long for him," Jake's wife, Stefany, told me. "Even though Sage is not physically with us, we can still do things as a family like go to a movie, go on vacation, and laugh and smile again, because he's experiencing these things with us in a different way. The whole family is healing, but Jake especially is."

When a person carries burdens, fears, or other negative emotions related to a loved one's passing, Spirit likes to suggest an effective exercise that I'll pass on to you too. They'll say, "Visualize me standing in front of you, with a suitcase open at the bottom of my feet. Put all the negative burdens that you carry connected to my passing inside, close the suitcase, and hand it back to me with love." There's no use for this baggage in the physical world—Spirit knows this, and you do too, deep in your own soul. So the next time you're weighed down by guilt, shame, or regrets, give Spirit's suggestion a try. They want you to lighten your load while you're here, and the Tricky Trio can be seriously heavy cargo.

20

Take the *Grrr* Out of Anger

You know what really pisses me off? Anger! It upsets me that this destructive emotion can turn us into such foul versions of ourselves. And yet anger is also a very natural response to upsetting situations, especially a loss. Think of it this way—if you've ever been annoyed about missing a party, or blown your lid over the dog tracking mud into the house, it would be pretty insane not to lose your shit over the devastating death of a person you loved very much. You know? Some people act like anger is wrong or bad, but Spirit says it's a normal reaction that happens to the best of us. It's when you keep the emotion inside, ignore it, judge it, hold on tight, and vow to get even that anger becomes harmful. And while you may not choose to feel anger, you do choose how to deal with it and whether to let it eat you alive or, as Spirit prefers, fix or accept the cause and release the hurt.

In the Heat of the Moment

Anger is an intense and powerful emotion that can also feel scary when it comes on strong or spins out of control. It can affect who you are and how you live. Because it taints your whole life, anger can also have far-reaching affects on your moods, how much you eat, how you heal from an illness, how fast you drive, how you treat the waitress at Applebee's, and on and on. The extent to which you feel anger can be surprising too, because at first, you might think of it as a familiar emotion, and yet it changes shape and size depending on the experiences that trigger it. The anger you feel after a spouse's death, for instance, doesn't feel like the anger you have when gas prices go up, because each is muddied with their own layers of sadness, anxiety, and fear—and even then, the fear of expensive gas eating your monthly budget is different from the fear of sleeping alone at night or raising kids on your own. And while it feels liberating to blow off steam, occasional venting can turn into regular tantrums and riots if you're not careful. You want freeing? Learn to manage your anger, so it doesn't trap or define you.

Much like blame, anger craves a target. It is a pointed arrow in need of a bull's-eye. When you're grieving a death, Spirit says it's common to direct your irate feelings at doctors, yourself, and God. You might even get mad at the person who passed and "left" you, which makes you feel abandoned and out of control.

But no matter who or what stirs your pot, Spirit wants you to know that getting past anger is a realistic goal. And in the meantime, when your blood boils, finding a "healthy" target might help. I like screaming, shouting, and punching a pillow until you're covered in feathers to get negative feelings out. Crying can also release anger, as well as the pain and frustration that feed it.

Have you ever been so mad that you start bawling? Me too! Sadness and anger overlap sometimes. I have a friend who lost her mom as a child, and when she gets mad thinking about it, she puts herself in situations that elicit a good cry, just so she can feel the emotional release. It's cleansing and empties her heart of all the frustrations she's stored   like clearing your history on the computer. She'll go to a tearjerker of a movie, look at old photos, drive past her mom's favorite park, or listen to a song that brings back poignant memories. These activities make her sob like crazy, but she feels significantly less angry when she's done.

That said, making yourself smile and laugh by rewatching a chick flick like *How to Lose a Guy in Ten Days* or a stand-up act on YouTube can alleviate anger and sadness too. Soul-soothing exercises like prayer, meditation, deep breathing, hiking, and playing with animals work well for more Zen personalities. I like to lift weights at the gym or take a Zumba class to release stress, but any kind of physical activity like running, boxing, tennis, or scrubbing dishes are productive ways to let out aggression too.

Spirit says death can cause you to feel helpless and powerless, because you probably didn't have a say in when your loved one died. As a result, you may feel the need to gain ownership over a situation, since death has made you feel like a victim. You might also spit nails, which feels warranted, and few would ever question or confront your outrage when they know about your deepest pain. For these reasons and more, Spirit shows me that anger is an easily accessible emotion that you might turn to after healing from depression and denial, even if it resurfaces in a lesser form. But just

> *If anger were a person, it would be the worst kind of frenemy—a familiar companion that's truly your rival.*

because this stage feels comfortable, that doesn't mean it's safe. If anger were a person, it would be the worst kind of frenemy—a familiar companion that's truly your rival.

A Spiritual Look at Anger

When anger gnaws at your soul, you become less of the loving person that you and Spirit know you to be. And if you don't manage your resentments and embrace life, you'll compromise your happiness and lose your way on your path. By following anger's lead, you'll enter the Other Side with extra lessons to learn.

I was taught that you can't have faith *and* fear in your life, which is interesting because both have close relationships with anger. For instance, a seemingly unfair situation can shake your faith in a just God, and this can make you angry at Him. Fear and anger can also mingle on their own, without lacking faith. I've noticed that if I'm anxious about work, I'm snippy to everyone around me, and it happens because I'm afraid that I can't handle what's on my plate.

Speaking of complicated feelings: Once on *Long Island Medium,* I read a woman who lost her fiancé in Super Storm Sandy. The man was sitting in his parents' living room, watching television, when a tree fell through the roof and killed him. The woman hadn't felt his soul since he died, nor had she dealt with how angry she felt about his absence and her having to raise a child alone. As a result, the woman stayed in bed most days, didn't take care of her health, spent very little time with her daughter—and then totally flipped out during our reading. As I was explaining how Spirit's signs worked, she screamed at her fiancé's soul, *"SHOW YOURSELF!"* Whoa, Nelly. I'd never had a client do that before (or since), and I remember wondering if the way she antagonized Spirit was similar to how she and her fiancé communicated when he was alive. Regardless, Spirit didn't want this woman to be so infuriated, since it affected how she and her child lived. It caused her to emotionally and spiritually retreat from everything that once mattered, because anger distorts and discolors your view of the human experience.

Though Spirit doesn't get mad, I have felt them express disappointment and concern. I only work with souls that are at peace in Heaven, but they still channel with the personalities they had in the physical world and can sound annoyed or short-fused if that was their way on earth. They'll also tell you when they're bothered by your behavior so they can help you make better choices and be happier. If you ever see me channel a perturbed soul, you'll notice that my voice becomes stern, since I'm feeling the message's intensity—the aggravation isn't coming from me. I once read a son whose father urged me to say, "Knock off the drinking." I sounded flustered, but that would be Dad's personality. His tone was like, *I know what's going on, so get it together.* And while his soul was blunt, I've conveyed the same request in a gentler way, if that's Spirit's agenda. I might say something like, "Please stop self-medicating." Big difference, I think!

So is there an upside to anger? Off the top of my puffy head, you could use it as a motivation to lobby for a cause or bring awareness to a misunderstood health condition. But again, when anger is used in a negative and/or destructive way toward yourself, another person, or a person's property, Spirit says it's just dangerous. And if your anger goes unresolved, it can lead to bitterness and resentment that damages your relationships, health, jobs, and enjoyment of life.

Control Anger, Before It Controls You

Long-term or extreme anger is most problematic when it's repressed, projected, or displaced. These actions can result in beating yourself up, acting critical, mean, or vindictive, and pushing people away when you could use their support. Untreated anger can lead to bad habits like smoking or drinking, or extreme gestures that feel justified, like taking the law into your hands if a person wasn't held accountable for a crime, rather than go through appropriate channels.

When you're angry, Spirit says it only hurts you to compare your indignation with another person's. Some are slow to anger, while you might go from zero to sixty in a hot minute. And while it's healthy to talk through your anger, you probably shouldn't overly talk about it. Everyone grieves differently, and a lot of people find peace with therapists and support groups. But they're not for everyone, or may only be helpful to an extent, because these settings might ask you to revisit anger and sadness by retelling stories that deeply upset you. As a result, you might bang on the same negative drum, over and over, until it becomes the hostile rhythm you live by. Such deep-seated anger will affect who you gradually see yourself to be, even if it's not who you are.

Another potential problem with oversharing is that you tend

to tell your story to people who you think will understand, but because they're not you, they may not. That's maddening! When I read a woman whose daughter was shot to death, she told me how she had tried a support group with other moms whose children had been murdered because it seemed that they'd have this life-changing tragedy in common. Yet no two moms were alike in how they felt about their loss—or even how to prevent similar disasters from happening to other families—and it made my client feel even more angry and alone than before. In the end, she was better off sharing her experiences with only a handful of like-minded friends.

> *Deep-seated anger will affect who you gradually see yourself to be, even if it's not who you are.*

Don't Get Mad, Get Healing

You can't wake up one day and decide not to feel angry. But there are constructive ways to work through bleak and hostile emotions and what causes them. With a death, I've noticed that admitting the finality of it helps; particularly with grief-related anger, hearing a loved one speak to you as a soul is a major reality check. Not for nothin', but you can't fight what happened or pretend it didn't, when Uncle Jim says he celebrated his birthday with you from Heaven.

I feel like Spirit's beef with anger is that it doesn't solve anything, not here or on the Other Side, so all the more reason for you to try to move past it. As with guilt and regret, Spirit often says to clients, "Let go of the anger and bitterness, and send me any negative emotions." But when Spirit asks you to hand over heavy burdens, or even questions your anger, please don't think they're chastising you. Even if Spirit had actual fingers to wag, they wouldn't *tsk–tsk* with them, because their best intention is to help you fully realize all you were meant to be and learn. They simply want you to control your anger, before anger controls you.

> Control your anger, before anger controls you.

I know how vicious and all-consuming anger can be, so I'm relieved when Spirit gives you compelling reasons to heal. During a show in Atlantic City, I read a woman named Leslie, whose husband, Edward, died from advanced heart disease on December 31, 2012—yup, New Year's Eve. And can you believe he proposed to her on the very same date, twelve years earlier?

Just before Ed passed, the couple had an incredible day with their two sons, one of whom was six weeks old. And that night, Leslie and Ed went on their first date since the baby was born, to a beautiful anniversary dinner and Coldplay concert. They were home early, chatted in bed, and Leslie made Ed rub her feet before falling asleep. They took turns feeding the baby through the night, and at six-thirty a.m., Leslie helped Ed prepare the bottle and went back to bed. Soon after, she heard a strange noise through the monitor, went to the baby's room, and found Ed in cardiac arrest and her son on the floor by Ed's feet. Doctors pronounced him dead at the hospital, though Ed's soul showed me that he crossed over at home.

"Ed and I were very much in love and very close, best friends, soul mates," Leslie shared. Spirit told me she'd been struggling with a lot of anger about Ed's death, though she's received encouraging signs and messages since he passed. My favorite is that on Ed's birthday, Leslie heard their wedding song, Chaka Khan's "Through the Fire," followed by Coldplay's "Viva La Vida." When do you ever hear those back to back on the radio? They were released twenty-four years apart! And during my live show, Ed piggybacked four messages for Leslie before I ever delivered his personal one.

"He wants you to know that he's so sorry for the day he passed," I told her during her reading. "If he could change it, he would, but he can't." Ed's soul meant that he couldn't alter what's already occurred, but I also suspect that a lesson about anger was attached to Ed's passing since the date of his death felt awfully specific. Leslie said she was mad that Ed died and left their family, but felt especially angry that he passed on their anniversary, which had always been attached to special and important memories. She was also jealous that her infant "got Ed's last moment," and not her. I felt that it was incredibly hard for Leslie to reconcile her fury at the time, and legitimately so, since she was dealing with postpartum blues and exhaustion, on top of the worst tragedy she's ever experienced.

I wouldn't wish Leslie's painful lesson on anyone, but things are looking up. "I waited half a year for an apology I never thought I'd get," she told me, as her reading happened nearly six months to the day after Ed died. "For Ed to say that he was sorry was huge for me. Nothing can make the situation better, but those words certainly helped and healed things a bit." At the end of her reading, I told Leslie that it's fine to feel furious and that she's not alone in her regret—Ed too was "grieving" in his way. While I knew his soul was happy in Heaven—nobody ever says it's bad there!—Ed's soul made me feel that it hurt him to witness Leslie's heartache and know what a difficult time she's had without him.

There's nothing quick or simple about resolving anger of any kind. But Spirit says that the better you get at learning to face and deal with your hurt, the closer you'll move toward the calm you deserve. Isn't it worth it?

21

Live a Little—Make That, a Lot!

When I'm distracted and overwhelmed, I'm more likely to carpe cannoli than carpe diem. It's so much easier to seize one good dessert than make the most of my whole day. But this is a lesson I'm working on, as should you. Actually, maybe you should consider embracing life as if it *were* a cannoli! Let's see . . . your journey would be the flakey shell, your lessons would be the mascarpone cheese, and your delicious memories would be all those tiny chocolate chips! Sprinkle the entire treat with powdered sugar, a.k.a. love, and that's a very sweet life!

As a medium, I've seen so many people carpe diem after a tragedy, crisis, or illness, but listen to me—don't wait for a painful situation to strike first. Spirit wants you to become aware of what brings you happiness and satisfaction *now*. Luckily, this isn't as vague or as overwhelming as it sounds. Simply notice how your body and feelings naturally respond to what you think and do as you go about your day—during meetings, playdates, drinks with friends, or downtime with a good book or Netflix rental. The more in touch you are with your responses, the easier it will be to interpret them and fill your time with rewarding activities and interactions. Before you know it, Spirit says you'll be a pro at navigating social, spiritual, and emotional situations. And you'll feel amazing about the outcomes!

Free Your Mind, and the Soul Will Follow

I talk a lot about how soul-searching can guide you to your purpose and on your spiritual path, but Spirit doesn't want you to obsess so much about growing your soul that you forget to enjoy the here and now! Especially since the easiest way to honor your spirit is to do what makes you happy (without hurting yourself and others). Filling your body, time, and mind with positive stimuli will help keep your soul in check. Spirit says it's essential to hang around people who make you laugh and feel good about yourself. For instance, don't invite friends to a party because you feel obligated, or neglect boundaries with challenging family, or cram your Saturdays with only chores. I know a woman who says she feels gross, anxious, and dumb after watching aggressive reality TV for too long; this kind of influence may not harm everyone's souls, but it strikes an unpleasant chord with her, so she stays away. Just like doctors say pain is your body's way of telling you that your health is off, Spirit says feelings are your body's way of sending a signal from your soul.

Some people have trouble determining when their efforts help or hurt them. For example, innate nurturers love looking out for friends but can feel exhausted and overwhelmed, or internalize others' sadness, if they're not careful. I once read a woman who dropped everything to care for others when they needed help, which is what she did as her mother was sick and dying. Yet when her mom departed and I channeled her soul, Mom didn't tell her daughter to stop helping other people altogether, even though it was draining. "I would not want my daughter to change, because it makes her happy to help out," her soul said. "She does it because she wants to, not because she has to." Instead, Spirit suggested that every time this woman did for others, she should do a little for herself. So the next time she took her elderly neighbor for her weekly hair appointment, she got a pedicure at the same time. And when she brought magazines to a sick friend, she grabbed a pizza on the way home so she didn't have to cook for her family that night. Her mom's soul said to her, "You can still be useful and take care of yourself"—which seemed like a no brainer to me, but it wasn't for my client! "Theresa, I never thought helping others could be like that," the woman said. "I thought I had to do all or nothing, or else I wasn't doing it right." Ever since, balancing her needs has made her feel more fulfilled than running on empty (go figure).

Spirit places people and events in your path that offer opportunities for joy and learning, usually at the same time, though we may not see it that way. I'm always amazed at how many lessons are rolled into a happy event. Whether you do for others or yourself, the moment can teach you to have faith, feel grateful, embrace love, forfeit your anger, and more. So treat yourself to a massage and give up your seat on the train. Soulful carpe diem moments are everywhere.

Living in the Now and Then

Spirit likes when you live in the now, but they don't want you to stop honoring the past or looking ahead. It might sound complicated to manage all three, but it's not. In fact, Spirit says remembering good times, realizing there are no accidents, and using your intuition are effective routes to living to the fullest, because you'll reflect in a positive light and adjust your attitude for the future. Of course, you don't always have to think so hard about this. Existing in the moment can be very gratifying on its own. Some of my best memories caught me off guard or occurred when I wasn't expecting them. Like as a young mom, nursing my babies forced me to stop, be still, and realize how much I loved my family, and living close to the shore has always reminded me to remain in awe of nature's magnitude.

You'll also recognize powerful moments more, as you become increasingly aware of your feelings and reactions as they occur. Spirit says everyone knows, deep down inside, that we deserve to have wonderful, love-centered lives—both intentional and accidental. But you have to open yourself up to them by putting yourself out there and trusting the guidance all around you.

I'll admit, it's hard for me to live in the now, but I try my best. I like to think of *ooh* and *aah* moments as God saying, "Hey, lady! Get a load of this! Slow down, smell the roses, and admire the sunsets, because life goes by real fast." When I was in Malibu, rushing to various meetings, my friend Rich who was driving pulled the car over on Highway 1 so we could soak up the gorgeous view. He knew we'd all benefit from taking five minutes to breathe, live in the moment, and not worry about whether we'd be late for our next appointment—and he was right. It was perfect! Listen, after years of dealing with chronic anxiety that forced me to plan every detail so I wouldn't lose my mind, Spirit's shown me that it's mentally and soulfully nourishing to experience the unexpected. Now I don't have to know what's going to happen next. A bump in the road is fine.

Living in the moment doesn't just go for reveling in laid-back experiences. When I'm dealing with a manic, full schedule, I find that if I focus on what I'm doing at that exact time, I'll enjoy it more and do a better job than if I try to juggle or guess what comes next. Maybe this is one reason Spirit gives you messages you need at that exact moment, instead of what you want or anticipate. They know that if you're always looking ahead or back, you can't focus on what's in front of you, and that's essential to happiness and growth.

I have to be in the now when I channel, which might further validate that this mindful state is connected to the soul. My anxiety got better when I slowed down and felt my feelings, which then helped me connect with Spirit. To feel normal again, I had to recognize what I was hearing, feeling, and sensing so I could release the energy in a productive and healthy way. I had to stop, breathe, and embrace the moment. I think that's an incredibly useful tool for anyone.

I Surrender!

You can't live life to the fullest if you're distracted and worried about heading in the wrong direction. When you feel defeated and think it's time to try another way, that's when Spirit wants you

> *When you feel defeated and think it's time to try another way, that's when Spirit wants you to surrender.*

to surrender. Only you can decide when it's time to turn the page, but you'll feel so tired from trying every angle without anything working out that you'll know when it's not meant to be. God doesn't want you to slam your head against a wall, but that's usually the point we let ourselves get to before we change our plans! Once you surrender to a new agenda, or simply trust the unknown, your soul will begin to heal and providence unfolds.

One reason surrender is hard is because it usually happens after you've invested a lot of time, sweat, feeling, and sometimes money into a meaningful idea or pursuit. It's hard, then, not to see surrender as giving up, failing, wasting time, or ignoring what you felt was meant to occur. But Spirit shows me that when you surrender, none of the process that preceded it was a mistake. Among other reasons, it's a lesson in courage to let go of an effort you've worked at, improved on, and tried to make right. It takes a big person to say, "I can't do this anymore. This situation is so much larger than I am. God, it's in your hands now."

Spirit says certain complicated situations are designed to challenge the control we think we have in life. It can also be hard to reconcile the fact that God gave us free will but not always total control! This double-edged sword becomes a valid confusion for

> *It takes a big person to say, "I can't do this anymore. This situation is so much larger than I am. God, it's in your hands now."*

people who swear their intuition led them down one path and it turned out that another was part of the plan. When your heart is set on a goal, and Spirit sends signs that you're on the right road until you're not, it's hard to change course. Even more confusing is trusting the new direction. But you have to understand, the time and energy you spent going the other way wasn't in vain.

What's more, Spirit says that when you muscle through a situation that leads to surrender, the lessons and gains are so much more specific and important than "what doesn't kill you makes you stronger" (though that's true too). You may have met people who will play a significant role in your life, or somehow developed your character in more effective ways than you would have on your own. The "wrong" path might not have even been about you—it may have been for loved ones. The outcome of your choices always affect other people, so perhaps all the players weren't ready for it to happen. The far-reaching effects of just one choice or decision in your life, no matter how major or inconsequential, would blow your mind if you knew about all the intricate inner-workings of the spiritual world. What you need to trust, then, isn't just this different path but that Spirit's got this. God, your guides, angels, your loved ones—they work hard to bring your best interests to fruition.

Knowing when to let go, sooner versus later, is a lesson because clinging to anything is a beeline to suffering. It is an act of desperation. When you struggle, it's tempting to hold on to a memory or situation, because it's familiar and you're afraid of the unknown

> *Knowing when to let go, sooner versus later, is a lesson because clinging to anything is a beeline to suffering. It is an act of desperation.*

alternatives. But there's a lot that God takes care of without your urging. The freakin' world spins on its axis without your help.

Listen, I'm not saying don't change what you have the power to change. But learn to notice when situations can't be changed. When you're swimming upstream, frightened and anxious, try to see when letting go is the best idea. This doesn't even have to relate to a life-changing catastrophe; you could simply feel better by surrendering to the fact that your alarm never went off, you got a late start, and now your schedule is delayed. To feel peace, you must accept things as they evolve. Spirit's sign for surrender is the throwing up of hands—like when they talk about fighting over an inheritance or surrendering to an illness. Their attitude seems to be that if it causes more harm than good, it's not worth it.

Call me morbid, but I think that surrendering to a disease is a terrific metaphor for any surrender in life. When you're incredibly ill and no longer fight death, you don't give up—you let go. You embrace what you've experienced and choose quality of life. It's a peaceful, positive, and concerted decision. I once channeled a mother's soul who said to her husband and daughter, "I want to thank you for letting me choose when and how to let go." After a series of cancer treatments, she and her family decided not to prolong her life but to travel the world. It meant so much more to create those incredible memories than sit in a hospital room watching chemo drip into Mom's veins. She and her family surrendered to her illness together, and as her soul said, "I died on my terms." I'm not saying you shouldn't fight like hell when you can, but when conceding makes you feel peaceful, content, and empowered, it's certainly worth considering.

Ultimately, surrender means releasing an image of how you thought things should go and accepting what life brings you instead. If you've visualized and prayed about this, know that Spirit's listened to and seen your hopes, but it's time to change your visualizations and prayers. Think about what you were once imagining, and then picture yourself handing it over to God or other Spirit. Then pray, "I'm putting this situation in your hands, so please guide me to the best choice and reassuring signs." Do not pray, "When you let me hit three green lights in a row, I'll know it's time to change course." Spirit says comfort and encouragement will come, but more likely as gut instinct, a conversation, a song, a sense of knowing, or another clear sign. You must also be ready for the answer, even if Spirit sends you one you don't like. It's best not to ask for guidance related to surrender until you're ready to make a change and stick with it.

You might initially feel or assume that surrender takes away your power, but it actually gives it back because you're choosing to relax and let life do its thing. But it's not just a need for control

> *It's best not to ask for guidance related to surrender until you're ready to make a change and stick with it.*

that makes it hard to surrender. Sure, this dynamic can be part of the fear because everyone likes to feel in charge of their life, and to an extent, that's justified. But there aren't many situations that we hold on to, for any reason, that are so easy to explain away. Spirit knows this, I know this, and I'll bet your therapist knows this too! So when you choose to surrender, be kind to yourself in the process and move at your own pace. Listen to your soul. I promise that once you alter your approach, and welcome your new flow, you will gain a fresh perspective that makes carpe diem feel like the amazing gift it is.

22

Miracles Are for Real

I'm not the type of person who takes bumper stickers seriously, but when I saw one that said MIRACLES HAPPEN, I was this close to having a Grey Poupon moment with the car's driver. *Excuse me, sir, do you happen to have any miracles?* Listen, he might have had connections worth asking about!

Not that I need a spiritual scoop from a stranger. My guides show me that miracles happen all around us, all the time, but we tend to overlook or underappreciate them. Miracles can also be misunderstood, and maybe this is because we don't know what to look for. Spirit's explained to me that a miracle is an event that defies reason and can be attributed to heavenly intervention. It might come from a healer, a saint, a higher power, or some other divine soul; you might watch it unfold or be part of it, and then find out later (say, in a dream) who delivered it. I believe all miracles start with God, even if other agents carry them out.

Miracles are rarely logical and often seem to buck the laws

of nature. We like to use the term "miracle" when someone survives a brush with death, like during an accident, natural disaster, life-threatening situation, or terminal illness, but miracles can also manifest as signs, a conversation, or any major event that changes your perspective. Spirit says that what makes a miracle a miracle isn't just the moment itself, but how it affects spiritual growth. And contrary to popular belief, miracles don't change when we die but how we reach our destiny. Spirit says that when we die is generally set, but a miracle can influence the degree to which you celebrate life and follow your path in the physical world.

I'll Show You a Miracle

A miracle is the highest form of spiritual intervention that a person can experience while here on earth. And though a fascinating or impressive miracle feels awesome and makes for a great story to tell your bowling team over beers, what matters most about the miracle is its spiritual significance. I'm all about embracing life to be happy, but miracles are an exception to the rule. Look, if God grants you a miracle, you better believe you should recognize the source and think about why you were blessed this way. Miracles aren't puny party favors given out for just existing, and you don't get them very often. Miracles are special and significant and pretty freakin' incredible, so don't act like they're no biggie, because they are.

Miracles mark a defining moment in your life and soul growth, because they take you to the next level of learning on your journey. A miracle brings you closer to your higher self and further along on your spiritual path. These phenomenons are directly tied to your most profound lessons, so the miracles you experience will be very different from mine and your neighbor's.

Miracles rarely fit into neat, cute, or generic categories. Take brushes with death,

Miracles mark a defining moment in your life and soul growth, because they take you to the next level of learning.

for instance. If you're a stuntman by trade, risking your life every day on the job is hardly a series of miracles. But if you survive a terminal diagnosis, now there's a miracle that might cause you to reevaluate relationships, renew your faith, or consider a new calling. See the difference? Or when people refer to having a baby as "the miracle of birth," unless the actual delivery defies odds, it's more likely that what we gather from parenting—novel views on love, patience, generosity, and so on—are the true miracles, since they trigger shifts in learning.

All this talk of miracles reminds me of an early episode of *Long Island Medium* in which I read a grandmother who'd lost her young daughter. God showed me that after years of praying that He'd "give her back," the daughter's soul reincarnated as the woman's granddaughter! When I followed up with the family, Grandma told me the reading changed their lives. She and her granddaughter were now extremely close, and everyone in the family felt more compassion for Grandma's story. The miracle wasn't so much that the daughter's soul reincarnated so soon—that was new for me, but it's also the circle of life (albeit, a sped-up version). The miracle was hearing that the reincarnation enhanced the family's relationships and increased their spiritual awareness.

As I was working on this chapter, Spirit specifically told me that "miracles are from another dimension." I interpret this as a validation of their divine origins and the universe's scale and magnitude. In other words, when your breast mass disappears after seeing a healer, your doctor doesn't get to blame a faulty mammogram— the healing came from a celestial place.

We've talked about how blessings also begin with God, cause you to recognize His guidance and influence, and are meant to be shared with others for encouragement. It's no wonder, then, that Spirit's shown me that life-changing blessings and miracles are related, because many small blessings can pave the way to a major miracle that takes you to a new level of growth. For instance, you might find a good parking spot at the mall during Christmas season (blessing), that leads to a perfectly timed run-in with a friend (blessing), who you tell about a shoulder injury from teaching aerobics, and this urges her to call a friend who gets you in to see the best surgeon in town (blessing). The *miracle* occurs, however, when after surgery you make a slow but full recovery and become closer to a son you rarely saw when you worked all the time. Maybe you also took an art class while healing, which felt meditative. Can you relate to this? You rarely see miracles coming, especially when they're the grand finale in a series of blessings.

Now that you know what a miracle looks like, it's so much fun to notice when God uses you to be part of someone else's miracle. At least I love when it happens to me! In a restaurant on Long Island, I read a man who was dying from liver disease. Though he was on a transplant list, Spirit urged me to tell him, "They're showing me a woman with black hair. Stick with her; she's healing you holistically." He told me this was his acupuncturist. Skip to a year later, and a new client came for a reading and said she found me through a referral. Don't you know, this was the acupuncturist with black hair, and she'd been referred by the man with liver disease! When I asked how he was doing, she said he was up for a fresh, new liver, but after a few initial tests, he learned that he wasn't even eligible because he's in remission. So for this man, hearing me confirm that Spirit was working through his acupuncturist was a blessing; the miracle was his healthy liver and learning how essential it is to have faith in the modalities you choose to heal.

Because Spirit uses my frame of reference to show me a message, I have to laugh that they compare something as ethereal as a miracle to the peppy Energizer Bunny—but they do! And the metaphor makes sense. When you experience a miracle, you're overcome with vigor, encouragement, and optimism that cause other great feelings like hope and faith. The positive energy is contagious, and its effects keep going and going! Spirit has also called miracles "God's cattle prod," since they're like an electrical shock that reminds you of God's power. It's like God saying, "Wake up! Get movin'! Life is good, see?"

So Are Miracles Part of the Plan?

We usually think of a miracle as an event outside of what's meant to happen, but the miracle is often written into your journey. This is because miracles inspire people to teach others what they've learned, pay it forward, and/or try to do or be more than before. So God knows that at some point in your life, you'll survive the

> We usually think of a miracle as an event outside of what's meant to happen, but the miracle is often written into your journey.

"impossible" and people will call it a miracle, but it was really part of a larger plan for you to talk or write about what you've learned. This will inspire, encourage, and renew faith. It will also act as the cattle prod Spirit talks so much about.

What's more, I've been shown that miracles can transpire when other people use free will to make extremely bad choices that could alter another person's path. For instance, Wendy, the nurse practitioner at my gynecologist's office, was attacked in a random act of violence as she was taking packages out of her car. The man stabbed her once with a fourteen-inch knife—the size of a bread knife or cake slicer—yet that single thrust tore up her body. Wendy remembers her struggle vividly:

> As soon as that knife went into me, I gasped and put my hand on my back. I felt a warm faucet of blood pouring out of me. I couldn't reach for my phone. I had a strong sense of clarity that if I laid down, I'd be dead. I staggered and crawled to my neighbor's house, and dove at her doorstep. She saw me from the window, and her son called 911. She screamed when she opened the door. I and her steps were covered in blood.

Wendy's recovery was in no way quick or easy. First of all, she underwent a six-hour trauma surgery. She lost her right kidney and a portion of her stomach; a major vein that carries blood to the heart, called the superior vena cava, was severed and needed to be repaired. Wendy was in the ICU for eight days, and when she got out of bed for the first time, she threw a dangerous blood clot. "I was told by the pulmonologist that they see this mostly in the morgue," she said. Wendy was then transferred to another hospital, where they performed open-heart surgery to remove the clot. She came home for a week, but returned to the hospital to treat an infection related to the initial stab wound, and shortly after that, had to be reopened to remove a piece of gauze that was left behind during one of her procedures. All told, Wendy was out of work for six months.

There were times that Wendy and her doctors didn't think she'd make it. Yet five years later, she has fully recovered, minus occasional inflammatory issues that are manageable with medicine, and Spirit told me this is because it was not Wendy's time to go. Her attacker used his free will to hurt Wendy, but it did not reassign her destiny in any way, because she'd not reached that window.

When I read Wendy five years after this ghastly incident, her parents' souls were anxious to communicate. From beginning to end, Spirit told Wendy that she was never alone during her ordeal. Her parents' souls said their energy literally transported Wendy's body to her neighbor's house that day, and their souls were in the room when her attacker was sentenced to fifteen years in prison. "Knowing mom and dad were with me gave me a different way of seeing things, which I feel is part of my journey," she told me later. "Angels are often left along my path to teach me how to see things clearer, which turns into gratitude."

Spirit also said Wendy's daughter, Corinne, prayed every night that her mom survive, and her prayers were answered. This struck Wendy, because Corinne was a teenager when their family's life turned upside down; she was afraid and, like many teens, coped with a "You'll be fine!" attitude that Wendy sometimes felt was dismissive or naive. She accepted it at the time, but after seeing Corinne cry as I conveyed Spirit's messages, Wendy was moved to tears herself. "I always knew Corinne loved me," she said, "but to hear about her prayers was heartwarming. We are so much closer now." The relationship that grew out of this reading was also a miracle, because it led to a stronger soul bond.

Although I don't feel Wendy's soul signed up for her miracle, she still benefits from what it taught her. "I can see what a truly horrifying experience it was and what a miracle it was that I lived. I was spared by God's grace," Wendy said. "I also know it was just a random act of violence, and I am healing. Today, I am, by far, the best Wendy I could be. I know my parents were with me through it all—mostly my mother, because that's what moms do! I have gone through many spiritual changes since that incident, and I'm convinced that all of the emotional and physical turmoil has brought me the peace and serenity I feel today."

Finally, it's no coincidence that Wendy feels compelled to share her experience with patients when it's appropriate; she also uses it to help them put their own negativity in perspective. "When I'm speaking with someone, and they start going into, 'I have to do this, I have to do that,'" she said, "I put my hands on their shoulders and gently say with a big smile, 'and then you get stabbed in your driveway and all bets are off, since life as you know it is put on hold?'" Gee, when you put it that way, your PMS and son's soccer schedule don't seem so bad!

Destiny's Wild

So again, while miracles change how we reach our destiny, they don't change when we die. Spirit says your destiny is part of your life plan, but how we reach that point is up to the choices we make in the physical world. I've never heard of there being a specific date that you're meant to die—it's more like a window of time—even if you choose to work in a job with a high mortality rate or go drag racing every weekend, which could affect your well-being but not necessarily determine how you pass. You can choose not to take care of yourself and not learn lessons and end up with sickness, pain, and unhappiness, but this would be counterproductive to your purpose, since you'd set yourself up to suffer. The better alternative, of course, is to lead a happy, healthy, and productive life, as well as spiritually evolve in the time that's been designated for soul growth.

Spirit tells me that death happens when that particular soul, not the human, chooses to leave—even if the body fights to stay alive when it's the soul's time to cross over. This reminds me of a reading I did during a live show in Fayetteville, North Carolina. Here, I read a couple whose son passed by drowning in a lake (you wouldn't believe how many kids I channel that die like this). Two weeks before the incident, he'd taken swim lessons, and that afternoon he tried to swim to a small island in the middle of the water where the older kids were hanging out. He took off his swimmies like a big boy, but he never made it to the island.

Spirit showed me that his father desperately tried to revive him, as his soul said, "Please tell my dad that he did breathe life into me and bring me back, but it wasn't my soul's destiny to stay." That's when the dad turned to his wife and said, "I knew he was still alive. I told you that in the ambulance." Most importantly, the child's soul wanted me to share how happy he is on the Other Side. "Tell my parents I can swim here! I can swim!" he exclaimed. He showed me how he likes to cruise to the opposite end of a crystal blue lake in Heaven—without his water wings, of course.

I love when Spirit teaches people about miracles by juxtaposing similar stories with different destinies. During a live show in Ottawa, Spirit led me to two women sitting near each other. The first had a niece who died when she was hit by a bus on a well-lit street; it was deemed a freak accident. Compare that to the second woman who was struck twice by a car, and upon the first impact, her soul actually left her body, traveled to the Other Side, and had a near-death experience. The car hit her body a second time, but this didn't impact her soul. Spirit told me she saw the Blessed Mother and angels, all of whom said to return to this plane, because it wasn't her destiny to die. With tears in her eyes, the woman told me that this is exactly what happened to her. So while the cause of each "death" was the same, the young girl passed because her time was up, yet the soul who was meant to do more in this world was literally sent back here by Spirit in Heaven.

Because miracles are in your path for a reason, God wants you to embrace them as rare and special gifts. When you get one, reflect on what it means in the context of your life. These are the "wow moments" that keep us going.

23

The Power to Heal Lies Within

After sharing my clients' lessons, messages, and stories—many uplifting, others heartbreaking, all inspiring—it's safe to say that I'm not giving away Spirit's secrets to a happy-go-lucky life! If that were my goal, I'd tell you to ignore your messy feelings, stuff yourself with ravioli and chocolates, and buy ten muumuus so you never have to button your pants again. No way! My ultimate hope, because it's Spirit's, is for you to have a healed life that completes your soul. This will help you realize that even your challenges have significance and meaning.

I know a few doctors who'd say that healing occurs when your physical or emotional health is restored, which allows you to function normally again. But when Spirit talks about healing, they're usually referring to your soul's restoration first and foremost—which can happen on its own or by way of improving your physical and emotional well-being. Spirit feels that healing your soul is essential, since it's the core of who you are and exists forever. Healing

> *Healing your soul is essential,*
> *since it's the core of who you are*
> *and exists forever.*

also tends to be an ongoing process, because you're always changing, and with that comes new and upsetting hurdles and setbacks. And unlike some doctors, Spirit doesn't consider you well, just because you can keep going. They want you to heal so you can feel vital, be your best, and squeeze every drop of happiness from life that you can.

Because a lot of us turn to God when we're upset or our bodies hurt, Spirit initiates emotional and physical healing too, but when they do, there is an equal focus on mending your soul for an improvement to your whole person. They don't seem to have a lot of interest in fixing one part of your body or just one problem, while other pieces of you suffer or unravel. Let's take an injured back, for instance. You won't truly feel better if you manage the pain with meds or surgery but continue to fight with your sister, which contributes to the condition. Or if you think about the emotional turmoil that comes with grieving, your sadness can't be resolved just by telling you a loved one is at peace; there's a good chance your grief is fed by fear, guilt, anger, or past dramas that deepen your sorrow, and those underlying issues need to be processed and repaired too. My point is: No physical, emotional, or spiritual disease (as some like to say) exists in isolation. Your body, mind, and soul are linked, and you have to mend all three to achieve balance, peace, and whole-body healing. And if you think you're an entirely healed and intact person, well, I'm sorry, but I'm not buying it. Unless you're, like, the Pope or Dalai Lama, in which case, you're probably in good shape.

Living Well

I was taught that we help create our health, which is another way of saying that your attitudes, beliefs, and values influence how you feel. This is hard for some people to hear or believe, especially if you have a disease or psychological tendency that seems hereditary. It might also sound like I'm blaming you for being sick or feeling down, but that's not my intention at all. Spirit has shown me that negative feelings like shame, anger, hatred, guilt, fear, grief, a lack of perspective, and an inability to forgive can contribute to illness and a failure to recover from loss or sickness. Do those categories look familiar? They should—they're Spirit's lessons! So yes, a resistance to learning can put the kibosh on all kinds of healing.

How you react to a situation or memory can also harm your well-being; seeing yourself as a victim of fate, circumstances, or God's injustice makes you feel powerless and can feed any existing sadness or medical condition. I think the worst attitude you can have is one of "damned if you do, damned if you don't." You set yourself up to feel stuck between two crushing walls, with nowhere to turn but inward. Before you know it, there goes your soul.

On the other hand, giving and receiving love, having a sense of meaning and choice, and feeling good about your journey will positively influence everything you do. As a result, having "a healthy lifestyle" doesn't only include eating well and exercising as most physicians or women's magazines would say. Rather, it's an ongoing and daily body, mind, and soul experience. In fact, Spirit shows me that you are always healing, even after you feel you've moved past challenges. Life is a lot like that game Whac-A-Mole that you play at the fair—just when you think you've beaten one furry bastard down, another pops up. The big hope, of course, is that as you learn lessons and become happier and more evolved, knowing how to overcome difficulties will become an intuitive response.

A Little Positivity a Day, Keeps the Doctor Away!

The link between healing and positivity isn't just a spiritual woo-woo theory; it's a well-established fact in the medical world. There's a lot of fascinating research that shows how optimists live longer than pessimists and have fewer emotional and physical health problems, less pain, less anxiety and depression, and increased energy. Yet a Debbie Downer personality type can riddle your body, mind, and soul with all kinds of problems. Anxiety, for instance, makes it hard to socially and emotionally function. It can cause you to doubt yourself, your sanity, and a higher power's presence in your life. And when it comes to physical repercussions, constant nervousness can wreak havoc on the gastrointestinal tract, musculoskeletal system, and every inflammatory condition out there. That's a whole body breakdown from one toxic feeling that spreads like a vicious gas leak.

I believe we're all born with diseases and disabilities, and that negative triggers can set them off or take your body past its tipping point. Spirit tells me that your emotions, and how you react to memories and situations in life, are some of the most powerful catalysts for illness and its proliferation. The good news is, Spirit also says we're capable of helping to turn this dangerous response off when we reply to a negative situation with positive intentions and efforts. Sometimes Spirit will ask me to do what I call a "body scan" during a reading, which is when I look at a person's body and part of it looks pink. This is my symbol for irritation in an area that's usually made worse by a stress or burden that needs to be released. Spirit then helps me guide the person toward naming the issue's cause and how to move forward medically, spiritually, and emotionally.

A lot of my clients have pink body parts, but I don't think negative feelings or memories are the only cause of dis-ease, though they always influence it. Genes, germs, environment, diet, and lifestyle choices are fac-

> *I believe we're all born with diseases and disabilities, and that negative triggers can set them off or take your body past its tipping point.*

tors too. Frankly, I don't feel there's ever one reason or solution for anything, whether you're talking about Spirit, sickness, or why my dad's freshly ground coffee tastes better than mine.

From what I can tell, negativity's effects on the body hardly seem that mystical, though the Law of Attraction is usually interpreted with a supernatural flair. I think that in many cases, the link between negative and positive energy, and how we heal, is pretty logical. Once I read a woman whose boyfriend died, and his soul was disturbed by the extent to which her grief controlled her well-being. In fact, when I delivered the message, she felt so bleak and bitter that she was full of justifications about why she couldn't heal, including that she was sick, depressed, and her relationships were failing. The lady had more excuses than Carter's got pills! Yet I sensed that she magnified her issues in her mind and chose to remain in a negative place that harmed her. Sure she had a real health condition and felt drained, but staying in bed, not eating well, and not getting fresh air or exercise made her symptoms and relationships worse. You can see how her negative perspective could bleed into her physical, emotional, and spiritual health in various ways. It wasn't a depressing vibe or universal magnet attracting bad juju that caused her life to fall apart. Listen, even if she'd simply responded to Spirit's messages with an open mind and heart, rather than angrily reacting to them, she would have taken a few helpful steps toward feeling better. You know what I'm saying? I truly understand how devastating death and illness can be—Spirit even goes to the extent of making me feel what you do, so I get it in a visceral way—but you have to try to make the good moments outweigh the bad as best you can.

The Way I See It

So much about healing has to do with perspective, so remember, your point of view is a choice. And when you decide to heal, you help create your wellness. You are responsible for your body, soul, and emotions, so when your health and happiness neglect you, you must find ways to get better. Sometimes you have to search long and hard for it, but never assume it's your burden to carry. Spirit says a lot is meant to be, but being an insufferable martyr is never part of God's plan.

> *A lot is meant to be, but being an insufferable martyr is never part of God's plan.*

Loss, disease, and other negative factors don't directly affect your ability to heal; what damages your soul is how you let negative factors affect you. Sudden death, a crippling accident, or an insulting boss are all terrible things, but how you react to them can be much, much worse. Instead, it's essential to feed your health with positive words and images when you're confronted with them. You become what you say and do, and that affects healing. I know a nutritionist who works with breast cancer patients, and she's noticed that as soon as they make their disease part of their identity—like playing the cancer card to get a good seat on an airplane or guilting their families into visiting on Sunday afternoons—their health swiftly declines. I can't be sure, but I suspect this happens because their words cause them to internalize their illness on a deep, soulful level.

On the other hand, Spirit tells me that when you're sick, believing in your treatments—meds, surgery, vitamins, juicing, herbs, whatever works—helps you get better, because you feel encouraged about your plan and have faith in it. Trusting your doctors can affect healing too. I also have to think that if you feel good about your choices, you're using your gut for guidance, and that's Spirit.

Sometimes when I channel a spirit, I may feel like they're healed when they passed, though the person clearly died. That's because their *soul* was healed when they reached their destiny. When I asked Spirit about this, they told me you can go through life with a disease, and even die from it, but still have a healed life because your soul came to terms with it. Interesting, right? No matter how you take care of yourself, no-

> *You can go through life with a disease, and even die from it, but still have a healed life because your soul came to terms with it.*

body lives forever. But Spirit says you can leave this world knowing you made the best choices and the most of your time here.

I'm always wowed when Spirit shows me what a great teacher healing can be. During a live show in Atlanta, I read a couple named Mike and Claudine whose daughter Brandi committed suicide her senior year of high school. She became very depressed when she broke up with her boyfriend and tragically hung herself after reading her ex's Facebook update that said he'd gone on a date with a new girl. When I channeled Brandi, her soul told me she'd found the peace she was looking for and assured her parents that they did the best they could. As disturbing as this is, Mike and Claudine have grown from their family's tragedy.

"As we slowly heal, we continue to learn about compassion," Claudine said. "We have more understanding and empathy toward others. Personally, this has made me a better wife, friend, and nurse. My husband and I have a closer relationship. We cherish every day and communicate better than before. We've made new friends that 'get us' and are all about being gentle, kindhearted, and saying the right things at the right times. We also have a good relationship with Brandi's best friend Leah, and we watch over her like a daughter. And as an oncology nurse, I relate better to my patients' feelings. Compassion touches every corner of our lives. We were good people before, but we feel this in a new way."

Yet no matter what kind of healing you seek, please keep in mind that Spirit tells me it's fluid. For most people I know and have worked with, there is no end point where you get to say, "All done! I'm better now!" You move two steps forward, three back, one more forward . . . and you carry on. As Claudine said, "We'll never stop grieving, but we do try to put our grief in a box and take it out when we've set aside time for it, so it doesn't rule our lives. Healing will be a process that continues until we cross over to see our dear, sweet daughter again."

One Heal of a Story

I wrote about my client Kristy in chapter twelve, but I wanted to share her healing story because her perspective and process were so intuitive, balanced, and astute, you better believe she saw a miraculous outcome. While learning lessons, she took a massive physical, emotional, and spiritual leap forward. Here's how she explained it to me:

> In 2010, as I was waiting for a double lung transplant, I held on to the belief that when the timing was right, I'd receive the perfect pair of lungs. After six months of stops and starts, I suspected I was blocking myself from accepting this gift. Shortly after I realized this, I overheard someone in pulmonary rehab talking about energy healing. I googled Reiki centers in my area and went for regular appointments for a little over a year.
>
> My practitioner gave amazing healings. Each one was a little different, but our mantra was always the same, "I accept new, perfect, pink, healthy lungs. My old lungs will come out smoothly and my body will accept the new pink lungs as if they were its own." With each session, I felt free to let go of all the worry about surgery that consumed my mind. Will the donor lungs be healthy? Will the incision hurt? Am I making the right decision? Am I hurting the donor family, wherever they may be? Can I let go of the lungs I was born with? Am I

going to die? Reiki helped heal my mind, relax my body, and let go of the fears and doubts that came from waiting for someone's body to die, so that mine could live.

My Reiki center also offered kinesiology, a natural therapy that uses muscle feedback as a stress monitor, to identify and correct imbalances in your structural, chemical, mental, and emotional energy systems. I learned that my body was living in a flight-or-fight mode, but with my surgical fears behind me, my kinesiologist helped me release the emotional fears that kept me from my "big ask." She suggested I plaster postcards all over my house with the mantra, "I accept new, perfect pink lungs freely and with gratitude." It was simpler than my previous mantra and included the spiritual component of ease and appreciation for my gift. As I taped up the final few, I realized how deep my pains were. They included a recent separation with my now-ex husband, and went as far back as growing up with cystic fibrosis and heartache related to my birth mother, as I was adopted as a baby.

I expanded my routine to include healing essential oils, meditation, visualization, and a lot more prayer. I'm Catholic, so it felt natural for me to pray to the Blessed Mother, Saint Jude, and Saint Anthony multiple times a day. My devotion was so pure, and I had unwavering faith. I believed that my guidance and friends who'd passed before me from cystic fibrosis, now angels, would lead me to where I needed to be. When I prayed, I always started with "thank you for my health . . . ," which sounds funny considering I was dying from a lung disease, but I thanked God for keeping me alive each day. I had eleven percent lung function, and I knew my body was hard at work to keep me alive. I then prayed for the donor family, that God would give them strength at the most difficult time in their life. I finally prayed for new, beautiful pink lungs. I also prayed novenas and the rosary every day. I prayed on my hands and knees on the days I could get out of bed and on the days I couldn't, I brought a Blessed Mother statue to my bedside and prayed to her all day and night.

I think it's important to say that I happened to have changed my prayers the morning I received the call that healthy lungs were ready and waiting for me. That day, I prayed that the Blessed Mother save me—not for me, this time, but for my mom. And if not, if God were going to take me to Heaven, I told him that I was OK with that because I now put the situation in His hands. In essence, my prayers became about others and the highest good according to His will. It's amazing too that my phone rang on December 8—the same day Catholics celebrate the Blessed Mother at the Feast of the Immaculate Conception. I had a hunch that if I were going to be saved, this was going to be the day.

When my transplant was over, the surgeon told my mom, "Kris received beautiful, new healthy pink lungs. We couldn't have wished for a better donor for her. The old lungs came out smoothly and the new ones went in perfectly." No one knew this was my affirmation, almost verbatim! I'd also visualized that my recovery would be quick, easy, and as painless as possible, and it really was. I had little scarring to the chest wall and sat up by day two and was home nine days later.

You know the saying, "It takes a village to raise a child"? I believe it takes many energy sources, coupled with your own *faith and desire to get well, to heal from physical, emotional, and spiritual ailments. For me, I didn't turn to one source of healing. I leaned on a "team" of doctors, God, angels, saints, Reiki, meditation, prayer, acupuncture, therapy, and kinesiology to bring me incredible blessings and a miraculous healing. Emotionally and physically, I was ready to accept my gift, and it arrived not a day longer or shorter of its divine timing. I had faith that healing would occur how, when, and even if it was supposed to—and I trusted the agents and modalities I believed in to grant it.*

Now Go Embrace Life!

The big moral of this book is simple: If you do your best to learn lessons, you will grow, thrive, and heal in the ways that you and your soul need. Be sure to meditate, pray, soul-search, visualize, look for signs, trust the voice in your gut, and follow your intuition to informed solutions—the suggestions work just as effectively when coping with a parent's sudden death to finding a good doctor or therapist.

My abilities are meant to help you heal and choose happiness for your life and your soul. Spirit insists that your time in this world is about cherishing the people and memories they place in your midst, however fleeting the moments seem. It's about knowing yourself well enough to create who you are and go after what you want, with the hope and optimism that each day will be better than the last—even if the last was pretty great. It's about trusting that Spirit, including God or a higher power, will help you along the way and never steer you off course.

It's no great secret that God didn't make me as eloquent as Mahatma Gandhi, so I wanted to end with one of my favorite quotes from him, since this peaceful Hindu leader basically says what Spirit shows me all the time. The only difference is that Gandhi uses the term "destiny" here to mean how you exist, not how you exit the world, but . . . tomato toma-toh. I love how he says . . .

Your beliefs become your thoughts
Your thoughts become your words
Your words become your actions
Your actions become your habits
Your habits become your values
Your values become your destiny.

How true is that? And while I'm not trying to one-up Gandhi here, as you now know, your soul's eternal experience doesn't end with your destiny in this lifetime. It's an ongoing evolution and the starting point for learning new lessons, from new stories, that collectively define our souls.

Afterword

Learning the Hard Way by Kristina Grish

In Theresa's first book, *There's More to Life Than This*, I wrote an afterword about the bizarre stuff that happened to my family while working on the project as her cowriter. My husband, Scott, and dog, Izzy, saw souls in our home, and I encountered Spirit through dreams, premonitions, and physical sensations. When we finished, Spirit explained their antics to Theresa. They admitted to heightening my intuition so I could experience what I was writing about and learn what it's like to live in her skin, since "being Theresa" on paper was my job. The process was one of the most unusual, fascinating, and spiritually rewarding experiences of my life.

So when we began writing Theresa's second book, I whipped out the sage before I even opened my laptop. I expected more spirited encounters and was curious to see what my guides had up their proverbial sleeves. But aside from fun signs while writing about signs (how ironic), *whooshing* sounds in my ears (this happens when Spirit is close to your body), digital recorder issues at curious times (like on the date 1/11 or at 2:22 p.m.), and noticing when my dog stared at our staircase for hours (Spirit commonly lingers there), nothing outrageously supernatural happened. Oh, I did have two precognitive dreams—one related to the book and the other to my home—which was super intriguing. But to be honest, I was hoping I'd wake up able to do a body scan or see a real, live angel in my garden. I'd even started a document called "Weird Shit," in anticipation of taking notes about strange experiences, but I rarely had anything good to put in it.

I realize now that I was foolish to think Spirit would raise my intuition with impressive psychic-ness, when that wasn't the point of this second book at all. It's about lessons. As soon as I acknowledged this, I had a sense of knowing that even before I met Theresa, the universe conspired to teach me a series of them, wrapped into one excruciating but worthwhile saga, so I could write with the awareness and sympathy of someone who's been there, felt that. This is to say, I feel Theresa's role in my life was at least, in part, related to the arrival of our first child.

Before I met Theresa, my husband and I, after navigating a terrible health scare and related infertility issues, were on a wait list for almost two years to adopt a baby girl from Ethiopia. When we began the adoption process, we anticipated an eight-month wait, but shortly after we submitted a mountain of paperwork, the program experienced changes that caused delays. Things happen, so we took this in stride as best we could. We kept up hope, laughed our way through a prebaby bucket list, and read books that adoption experts said would make us better parents. Time didn't fly, but we managed.

Then one afternoon I learned that the number of referrals coming out of Ethiopia was drastically cut, and my gut felt the very real and painful possibility that this might not work out for us either. I don't even recall what our agency's email said exactly, but I remember my reaction—I let out an intense wail and literally slid down the wall in my hallway. The windows were open, and I remember thinking three things: (1) the neighbors are going to assume my dog died; (2) I thought sliding down walls only happened in Lifetime movies, but I guess it's a real thing; and (3) I need a serious, major blessing or I'm going to lose what little faith I have left in God. Meanwhile, I'd seen *Long Island Medium*, loved the show, and was up for an interview to cowrite Theresa's first book. The night of the horrible email, I prayed to God, my Nana, and my cousin who'd just died, *If I'm not meant to have a baby now, I need this project to get me through the wait. Please help make it happen. I can't do this anymore.* A month later, I got the job.

During my first lunch with Theresa, we split a caprese salad and talked about our families. I mentioned that we were waiting to adopt a daughter from Africa, secretly hoping that Spirit had a date for me, or maybe a name. Here's what Theresa said: "A baby girl. Are you sure? From Africa? Hmm." She did that lip-biting thing. I was confused. She then told me her Nanny sent us a fat, hairy fly on the mirror behind me. This was before I understood how signs and reassurance worked (the fly was validation for her that she was on the right track), and I couldn't figure out her segue between thoughts. It scared me to think that one person could be so tapped into how the universe worked, and others, like me, could be so clueless.

About an hour later, Theresa became distracted a second time with Spirit and stopped, in the middle of a story, to let me know that my own Nana had something important to say about the baby. "She says you have other choices," Theresa told me. "And I'm sorry, but she's showing me a baby boy. You keep saying it's a girl, but I'm getting a boy. From America, not Africa." What was this woman talking about? Our decision wasn't up for further discussion. I must have looked like I'd heard from a mean ghost, because Theresa softened her approach. "Who knows? Maybe I'm wrong? But don't limit yourself," she said. "Just pray for a healthy child and visualize a flawless process. That's all that matters, right?"

I wasn't even a little relieved to hear her advice, the way most of Theresa's clients are when their dead grandmas give them healing messages. I was devastated, and frankly, I thought she was full of it. For two years, I'd visualized an African baby girl's birth and subsequent adoption—*my* baby girl's birth and adoption—and I'd even bought her a floral embroidered dress. I'd prayed for her soul and birth mother every night, and my husband had written a book inspired by the idea of her (which, one could argue, should have the same effect as manifesting). I swore that I felt her soul around me and received countless signs that the baby I'd imagined for so long would be part of our family. She was already very real to us, even though we'd never met her. As for her birth country, I felt deeply and passionately drawn to Ethiopia and their children—it just had to be a go.

Babies aside, I should be clear that I believed every other word, message, and story that came out of Theresa's mouth from the moment we met. She could have said I was a ghostwriter for the Bible in a past life, and I'd have been like, "Cool! Who was at the launch party?" And while Spirit unveiled outstanding validations about their presence and God's magnitude during our first book together—for Pete's sake, my husband saw dead people and I turned temporarily psychic!—I didn't want to accept that my own life-changing message was on target. Theresa may have been accurately using her abilities to channel Spirit for over fifteen years, but this one time, *with me*, I thought she was dead wrong. Pun intended.

Whenever Theresa and I met after that, I waited for Spirit to tell us they'd made a mistake about my African daughter. And when I had those thoughts, Theresa must have intuitively known because she'd try to nudge me toward Nana's advice, but with human logic like, "If you were giving birth, you couldn't choose sex. Why not a boy?" or, "Doesn't health matter most?" After a few months of this, she got blunt: "Listen, open up to a baby boy. His soul is waiting."

It took *another ten months* for me to listen to Theresa, sort of, and only because Ethiopian referrals slowed to a near stop. Other international adoption programs floundered. Scott and I felt that we had little choice but to adopt from the U.S. Just so you know, we had nothing against domestic adoption; we were just stuck on what we wanted, come Hell or high water. And after years of heartbreak and feeling hosed by a higher power, we felt entitled to a say on what our family would be. Adoption should be motivated by the best interests of children, but as prospective parents, it's hard to entirely ignore your desires; adoption seemed to give us options and a mild sense of control, though this was naive. Anyway, when we did switch tracks, I still didn't want to believe I wouldn't raise a daughter, so I told our agency we were open to either sex. I considered this progress.

When we changed course, I also tweaked the way I expressed my hopes to God. I stopped praying for my needs and began to thank Him, in anticipation and with faith, for our baby's birth mother and her incredible gift to us. I asked that whoever she is, that she feel intuitively drawn to choose us as parents for her child, and at peace with her decision. I prayed for the infant's health and that he or she (*please be a she, please be a she*) grow up to be wise, happy, productive, and kind. And I told God that whatever child is meant to be ours, I needed Him to make it so stupidly obvious that we couldn't ignore it. I put the situation in His hands, and then I waited for The Call. I'd say that eighty percent of these efforts sprung from faith and a good twenty from surrender and utter exhaustion.

The next time I saw Theresa, she said to me, "Spirit showed me the number fourteen is connected to your baby somehow." A week later—*and only three weeks after submitting our new paperwork*—we were matched with, you guessed it, a baby boy due on the fourteenth of that month. I was in shock. I went to my room and prayed for only the highest good of all concerned, and again, for the child's and birth mother's well-being. This wasn't even strategic; it just felt right.

Once we were selected, I've never felt so divinely guided in my life. It's like Scott and I were in a relay race, encountering invisible, outstretched arms that helped us, at every new turn, to reach our goal. Trust me—after spending so many years pushing against what I now believe were defining moments on my path, I will forever know Spirit's hand when I feel it. Our son's birth was remarkable, everyone was healthy, and our transition home went off without a hitch.

Reassuring signs also hit us over the head, although three seemed particularly special. When we arrived in the town where our son was born, the first cafe Scott and I spotted for lunch was called Mimi's. This is my departed cousin's name, the one who I initially prayed to, and whose last words to me were, "I'll help you get that baby from Heaven." Then, as we raced to the hospital as his birth mom was going into labor, out of nowhere a 1970s Pontiac Bonneville pulled in front of us at a stoplight. This is the car Scott's deceased grandfather drove and handed down to him as a teenager; Spirit always uses it as a validation during readings. Finally, my jaw dropped when we got home, and the wonderful baby nurse we hired for a week handed me her business card. On it was a picture of two open palms with light radiating from each.

So . . . yeah. Maybe the Long Island Medium was on to something.

My son was born when Theresa and I began writing her second book, which means I had to form coherent sentences while he was still a fussy infant and I was an exhausted first-time mom. Theresa and I had a running joke that sleep deprivation made it easier for me to channel its content—not that this was necessary. With almost every chapter, Spirit referred to the adoption as it related to the subjects we covered. It became quickly obvious that so much of my journey was linked to the lessons in her new book. Faith, patience, acceptance, blessings, intuition, prayer, anger, surrender, healing—my long trek to motherhood repeatedly fed our conversations. I realized too that Spirit's MO wasn't so different from how they heightened my intuition for her first book; once again, Spirit wanted me to relate to the subject matter in a personal way, so I could understand and communicate their intentions. And every time I'd think, *I can't believe I'm working so much, and so hard, when all I want to do is nap for a very long time with my baby,* a gentle voice inside would remind me to be grateful, and keep going.

"You received the most beautiful miracle," it would say. "Go get another cup of coffee."

Bouncing my son in the Björn one afternoon, while also taking notes on a call, I asked Theresa an important question: "So how can readers make the most of their lives, learn lessons, and fulfill their souls' paths without having a medium as a friend?" I was kidding around, but as the words flew out of my mouth, I realized they were purposeful. I kept them in mind as we worked, always praying to God, my angels, and my guides to help us bring you the lessons that would allow you to heal, learn, and grow as much as possible.

Despite everything I learned, I was still confused about why I'd felt compelled to adopt a daughter from Ethiopia if an American son was intended to be part of our lives. Spirit told Theresa that it was because I acted so stubborn about our choices and wouldn't have adopted a baby boy from the U.S. *unless* they took us on the scenic route. Yup, that sounds right. It was also fun to hear that our son's soul chose me and Scott as parents to help him learn some of his lessons in this lifetime. Finally, Spirit added that a girl's soul is still within reach—they showed her playing on a swing set, with God, my departed loved ones, and my angelic guide surrounding her—but she will be a choice for us. Our son was not, and I'm so thankful for that. I can't imagine my life without him.

Our adoption experience forces me to marvel at how long it took me and Scott to trust in a bigger plan and purpose. Looking back, I can't believe the extent to which we held on to what we wanted to believe was meant to be, rather than open up to new options when it became clear we were swimming against the tide. Theresa has said that the path of least resistance can be the most spiritual one, and in my son's story, that lesson is apparent. And though Scott and I suffered like hell in the interim, we gained a lot too. We met like-minded friends with Ethiopian children who are still a considerable part of our lives. We also tested the borders of our existing circle's patience, support, and compassion, and learned that they love us more than we knew. And then there were the Theresa lessons. Writing her first book renewed our faith, and changing adoption plans was about choice, surrender, and letting go. She played such an incredible (and painstaking!) role in guiding us to our child that it's no wonder I asked her to be a godmother.

Theresa sent me an email the other day, and a line in it really stuck: "My friends pay attention to everything I say because when I talk, they say it's like getting a reading, LOL!" I know it wasn't her intention but all I heard was, *Next time, save yourself a lot of grief and listen to me when I tell you something*. I'm such a big dummy. And when my handsome son flashes me his best, toothless smile, I pause to thank God for so much. From now on, I'm all ears.

May you learn from the emissaries who come from on high

May you come to understand that we never die

May you realize the purpose of life and your soul

May you begin to understand it's a lifelong goal

May you come to understand what lives for eternity

May you come to learn what can and cannot be

May you open your hearts to only know love

May you know what is earthly and what's from above

May you know of the angels that protect you each day

May you hear their guidance so you never stray

May you always be aware of God's love, protection, and light

May you offer Him thanks, each and every night.

—FROM THE POEM "MAY YOU" BY BILL MURPHY, 1946–2013

Acknowledgments

If writing this book has taught me anything, it's abundant gratitude for the people who love and support me in the physical world, and for Spirit, especially God, who sustain and guide me. Without any of this, I couldn't mature as an author or as a medium, and I wouldn't be able to help others heal and grow too.

A huge thank you to my amazing coauthor Kristina Grish for burning the midnight oil on this book. Your continued enthusiasm and ability to make sense of the "unique" way I think and speak led to a *New York Times* bestseller the last time we did this—now *that's* a gift. Here's to another!

To my editor, Johanna Castillo, and publisher, Judith Curr, for trusting my abilities, loving my stories, and encouraging me to put it all on the page. I'm thrilled that we found each other.

To my awesome manager, Courtney Mullin, whose direction and protection in every aspect of my career has helped me come so far and impact so many. Your devotion to me and Spirit is unwavering, and you've taught me to just breathe. I feel so blessed that you're in my life.

To Jonathan Partridge, who sure knew a telegenic medium when he met one! Thank you for your hard work, commitment, and effort through the years.

To my assistant, Courtney "CC" White, for brightening my days with a smile and song. You have the voice and heart of an angel. I'm lucky to have you. Thank you for showing me how to appreciate the small stuff and not sweat it.

To Victoria Woods, whose social media savvy has expanded my reach and makes me crack up all day. I'd never be able to Twitta without you!

To Magilla Entertainment and TLC, for your commitment to allow me and *Long Island Medium* to help people heal, one episode at a time. And to my amazing crew, I love and appreciate every one of you. You're like family to me; thank you for giving this show your all.

I also want to thank Rich Super from Super Artists and everyone at Mills Entertainment for making my live experiences such a success. I'm grateful to Michele Emanuele for keeping me in feathers and sequins, and to my attorney Jeff Cohen for always looking out for me.

To all my friends who've stood by me, especially Eileen Bacchi and Desiree Simonelli; even as our lives have changed, our friendship has not. And to Pat Longo, for your friendship, pride, and, yes, reality checks. Thank you!

To Regina Murphy, for giving so much of your time and heart to this book. I think of Bryan and Bill every day, and I know you feel their souls as strongly and peacefully as I do. I'm so grateful for you and for them.

To my extended family on both sides, especially Aunt Debbie and Aunt Gina, for standing by me no matter what this gift brought with it. And to my cousin Lisa Brigandi, who's still my favorite shopping partner. If anyone's taught me how to use a credit card, it's you!

To my parents, Ronnie and Nick, who've always made me feel

loved and secure with their actions and words. I want you to know that I am so proud and blessed to be your daughter. You've shown me faith, love, and happiness, but the most valuable lesson you've taught me is the importance of family, and that God places people in our lives for a reason and to help us trust in Him. I love you! I also want to thank my brother, Michael, and his family, for their genuine love, acceptance, and interest in what I do and what it means to me. I'm grateful too to my family in Spirit, including Gramps, Gram, and Nanny, for guiding and cheering me on. And to Connie, Jack, and the rest of the Caputos for giving me so much, including your secret meatball recipe!

To my husband, Larry, who is and always will be the love of my life. Thanks for riding shotgun on this crazy ride and holding down the fort at home. I've learned true, unconditional love from you. I'm so glad God's plan put you in my corner, because I couldn't do anything without you. And to my children, Larry Jr. and Victoria, I'm so proud of you! You've taught me understanding and patience (that last one's for you, V), and I hope you think having a mom who talks to dead people has worked out OK. I'm a good icebreaker at parties, right?

Finally, I'm forever thankful to God and Spirit for such a spectacular ability that allows me to do their work in the most fulfilling and enriching ways. And to my clients and fans, who inspire me every day with their resilience, trust, and open hearts. Because of you, I get to connect with incredible people and inspiring souls, and then call it my job. Dare I say, I feel so blessed.

xoxo,

Theresa